What Now?

From Dreading to Dreaming

SUSAN R. SCOTT

To My Grandchildren ~

Elijah, Benjamin, Abigail, Gabriel, and Emily:
You are inspiring me to dream again, and reminding
me how full of wonder ♡ life is really meant to be.

And to Their Grandfather, "Scottie" ~

After our first date (46 years ago), I started dreaming
of what it would be like to grow old with you. We still
don't really know what "old" feels like, but the growing
together part has been even better than I had dreamed.

Contents

Like holding a seashell to your ear
to hear the whispers of a vast ocean,
this book is only an echo of
the powerful Truth of God's Word.

"...seek and you will find"

~ Matthew 7:7

Acknowledgements

The author's name is on the cover but if there
were room, these names would be listed as well:

Editing Consultants ~

Kimberlyn Evers   **Christine McGrory**

Support Team ~

Sandra Kenneally   **Lynn Olmeadi**

Diana Lally   **Kathy Stanley**

Tara Mantho   **Jules Sweeney**

Lisa Mooradian   **Amy Szczur**

It's because of their prayers, ideas, and feedback,
(as well as the love and encouragement of other
dear friends and family), that the publishing
of this book was able to be completed.

INTRODUCTION:

From Here to There

I have a friend who has my contact information entered into her phone under "Sunshine and Roses." She's not being sarcastic, so I consider it a compliment. It struck me funny when she told me, and even funnier when I realized that her title for me fit perfectly (quite unintentionally) with my actual initials: S. R. Scott. My "sunny disposition" these days does not come naturally. It's only because God patiently explained to me (over and over until I finally got it) the importance of keeping my words and attitude positive. What we speak is incredibly powerful because His Holy Spirit has empowered our words with authority to create change. It does not mean living in denial or being inauthentic. It means taking thoughts captive before you speak them, or even mumble them, and only declaring words that edify or encourage. We can speak God's truth, speak His heart, bless our world, and spin things for good; or we can curse and destroy by agreeing with negative (sometimes demonic) ideas, or facts that only declare darkness. God's honest truth always trumps the facts of this world. He stacks our deck with such good things to declare, but leaves it up to us to choose which card we want to play.

Winning the battle to only speak life, does not come easily to me. I grew up with someone who saw most glasses half empty, and someone else who was afraid that a half empty glass could shatter at any minute. It's only by God's grace and enabling power that I can stay positive at all. Even though I want the glass to be overflowing, it's a daily mental and emotional wrestling match that I don't always have pinned down. So, it may surprise my friend to find out what really goes on inside of this "Sunshine and Roses" head of mine, each day.

What Now?

At the risk of breaking some of my own "keep-it-positive" practices, I'm going to be transparent with you in hopes of getting to the bottom of the dread many of us have been experiencing, especially lately. Maybe we can discover together what to do with disappointment, crushed hopes, and some of those stepped on dreams we've tucked away. We may have even *thrown* them away because of critical inner voices (and possibly those of loved ones) telling us we're just dreamers, get your head out of the clouds, or even more insulting: out of the sand. Can we somehow reignite our expectancy, and find the resolve to dig through the trash and rescue what we once treasured?

When "dream" turns to "dread," your circumstances and broken heart can pound like a persistent thumping mallet. You fear the next thump could be a fatal blow, but your feet are stuck to the ground and you can't get out of the way fast enough. The idea of "speaking positively" feels positively useless. At times, nightmares seem more real than God's promises, and the promises start feeling more like fairy-dust being blown away by those looming storm clouds.

How can reciting them make any kind of difference? For years now, I've wondered how, as many mornings I have awakened with dread for no good reason. I deny it, rebuke it, tell it to leave, and remind myself of God's promises. Some days I win right away; while other days it's more of a marathon. Speaking with others, I'm finding it's a common occurrence for many of us. Maybe by processing this together, we will overcome the dread instead of allowing it to overcome us. And our crumpled up, forgotten dreams might start to unfold again. Could it really be our time to turn "dreading" back into "dreaming?"

I'm ready to turn the page and find out. Are you?

1:

From Hype to Hope

The three generations that live in our household just survived not only all the hype of the 2020 global pandemic, but the actual dreaded virus itself. I'm convinced COVID-19 was released globally by dark forces to wreak havoc and steal hope. We had followed the rules and paid attention to the guidelines. We took precautions and stayed socially distanced; yet here we are. The symptoms we experienced were bizarre, and definitely felt manufactured and not just a natural occurrence. The emotional torment was actually worse than (what felt to me like) the "plastic" symptoms of the virus. The fear and uneasiness that accompanies catching it, swirls around and taunts everyone. It may have been all the media-hype and fearmongering, but it appears to profoundly affect many people psychologically as well. Whether all the conspiracy theories prove true or not, knowing God sits in heaven and laughs at the plans of earthly kings[1] consoles me, to an extent anyhow, and stirs up my hope that *His* justice will prevail.

As I write this chapter, I'm three weeks into recovery and I'm continuing to declare that the virus is treading illegally and must completely vacate this household and the rest of our world as well. I feel my spirit ever so slightly starting to rise up (well, maybe more like crawl up out of the mud) again. I've been asking God:

> *What needs to be learned from this? What needs*
> *to be stepped on, and what needs to be stepped over?*
> *As a trophy for enduring these symptoms, I was hoping*
> *that maybe You could give me a new perspective?*
> *A higher point of view, perhaps?*

---

[1] See Psalm 2:4

1: From Hype to Hope

It isn't a new request. I've been asking God for a while now to tear back the veil so I could see things from His perspective; so that my spirit would have more sway than my natural eyes, and I could impact my world more effectively — more truly. During this insane battle of shutdowns and panic-driven mask-mandates, He's given me a glimpse that the veil gets pushed back from *my* side. It starts by praying in the Spirit and keeping my mind focused only on the beauty of our Heavenly Father and His perfect love. The longer I think about Him, the more the curtain gets pulled back, the more in focus I begin to see, and the physical realm all but fay-Ah-Ah … Ah-CHOO! and the physical realm (with its viral symptoms) all but sneezes and blows the curtain closed again. Will I ever get the hang of trusting Him no matter how I feel or what it looks like? I know practice makes perfect, but how much practice are we talking about here? Little did I know, a higher perspective would come as a result of just trying to maintain my sanity. Fighting this virus has forced me into practicing day and night how to rise above my circumstances and how to look beyond what my physical senses are telling me.

What Now?

I know this new season we're in requires a new level of faith for all of us. This means being really sure of what we hope for and completely certain of what we do not see[2] or perceive with physical senses. It requires believing more in God's pure truth and beauty by gazing at His Sovereignty until everything else in sight fades away. For me it means immersing myself in Biblical descriptions of God's Character and hearing stories of His love repeatedly, until I envision Him gloriously surrounded by colors that are rich beyond this world — transparent, iridescent prisms of Heavenly rainbows and flashes of lightning — only visible when my eyes are closed and my heart (my spirit) is totally focused on Him. It's practicing *that*

How do you envision God?
How do you address Him?

_____

_____

_____

_____

_____

_____

_____

---

[2] See Hebrews 11:1

kind of "seeing," and intimate worship, that leads us higher and opens our eyes to give us a better perspective, more able to dream with Him and imagine for the impossible.

To operate in that kind of faith at a new higher level, we all have to step up, by stepping down. Okay, kids, looks like it's back to kindergarten time. No, I'm not talking about taking an afternoon nap (though that does sound tempting about now). It's just that we're all about to be put into the same grade, because God is doing a brand-new thing in all of us at the same time. God started months ago giving me fair warning that He was doing a new thing by compelling a very good friend of mine to text me Isaiah 43:18-19. It resonated as I read it:

Forget the former things; do not dwell on the past. See, I am doing a new thing! Now it springs up; do you not perceive it? I am making a way in the desert and streams in the wasteland.

The next day I circled it in my Bible, and Jesus and I laughed and laughed as I heard Him repeat, "Do you not perceive it?" like, "Hey, Silly-Susie, don't you get it yet? I'm doing a new thing!" And then it began: Almost every sermon I heard, prophetic word, devotional, or social-media post I read, contained Isaiah 43:18-19, or at least portions of it. He knows I

> *Do you sense anything new going on in your life, or maybe on the horizon?*

need to hear things more than once and from different angles before it actually sinks in. It still amuses me each time I hear God ask me, "And how about now? Do you perceive it *yet?*"

After this year of global reset, when the entire world has been panicked into isolation, careful reflection, and a restructuring of life, it appears there has never been a better time to all learn something new together (now that we're seeing the bigger picture globally, bigger than life and bit more clearly). It's as if this whole chaotic time of pandemic lockdown has set us up to actually want to jump out of the nest and soar again (into anything but the four walls of quarantine we've been staring at for months). Gliding on the winds of our past can sustain us for a while, but to catch the next thermal we really have to be willing to leave all of that behind. I normally need to be pushed out of the nest, but at this point, I think everyone is more than eager to say, "Good riddance!" to the old, perched right on the edge and ready to fly the coop.

I used to dream at night of soaring without a plane high above the clouds, hills, and valleys of the world below. Flying dreams are commonly interpreted as learning to rise above our negative circumstances, or simply feeling pretty hopeful and excited about life. Seems people have a lot more flying dreams as children. We're usually forward, positive thinkers when we're young. I haven't had a flying dream for a very long time. If our expectations are focused on our circumstances, or the people around us, we will be consistently disappointed and lose hope. But if instead we carry an expectancy of seeing the goodness of God in the land of the living[3], our hope can be restored. Throw away "expectations" — even those you have placed on yourself. Replace it with "expectancy" —

[3] See Psalm 27:13

hoping in a God who never fails. As you watch your strength get renewed, you might just mount up with wings as eagles.[4]

My 7-year-old grandson runs (more like flies), skips, and bounces just about everywhere he goes. I don't think I've ever seen him walk anywhere. I had a quick movie-like clip play in my head the other day of a full-grown adult entering and exiting a room with the same energy and maneuvers, and I laughed aloud. My grandson represents to me "dreaming with God" — full of life, hope, joy, and fun. Can I ever recapture that for myself? My 61-year-old *body* may not be able to emulate it, but can my soul?

I really think when Jesus says to become like a little child for to such belongs the Kingdom,[5] He's saying we need to be humble, not worried; to be like a child who is trusting, and who understands their life's purpose — just to play, to pretend, to giggle a lot, and to run like the wind. I could really use some of that right now, except the running part. Even as a child,

---

[4] See Isaiah 40:31
[5] See Matthew 18:2-4

running felt like work to me. But climbing trees? Now *that* was awesome! I loved being way up high, swaying with the breeze, above everything. I find myself wondering how to recapture and pull to the forefront that fearless climber who once ruled my outdoor adventures. What happened to that tree-top swayer, eager to try a new thing just to see what it would feel like. And here God is

> *Is there something you wish you could still do now?*

again, calling me to something new (even beyond writing this book), something that feels adventurous and as impossible as dreams can seem. He's telling me to trust Him, get excited and start climbing (or at least start dreaming about climbing).

I'm not sure exactly what God is about to do next. What I sense for now, is the chaos of transition and the mystery of a surprising event around the bend. But I feel like a character in a sitcom who has eavesdropped and mistakenly thinks there's a surprise party planned just for me. I keep peeking into potential venues, walking into rooms ready to act surprised, looking around corners expecting balloons and streamers, and asking, "Is this it? How about now? Is this the new thing? Did I miss it? What do You mean we're still in transition? Can't we just give birth already?" But transition is a vital time when God does something new in us, so we will be ready for the new thing He

Does a hopeful dream pop into your mind right away, or is it tucked so far back that you need a magnifying glass to make it out?

is about to do in the world. It is best not to rush through it. This transitional time is exactly what it takes to make us ready and willing enough to leap into God's sweet dream for us. All the times before when we gave up on it, let it slip away, or even ignored the dream altogether, have finally brought us to this place of overcoming the dread and surrendering to the dream.

1: From Hype to Hope

When God is your Dream-Giver, you can be at peace. Let the dream rest in your spirit and manifest in your imagination. The Designer of your destiny will begin to deliver more of His plan on how to get there, but only as much as you can handle at a time. Don't pay too much attention to any hesitation you feel or push back you experience. It's probably just your practical side kicking in and pointing out the impossibilities and "what ifs" of the dream. Just trust Him and anticipate the very best ideas and thoughts — the ones that make you smile expectantly. Our determination to embrace with faith those ideas, despite our feelings or what it looks like, is what helps a dream start to take root. Easier said than done though, right? After asking how to embrace a God-given dream that requires more faith than you think you have, someone recently suggested to me:

> That's easy. First you need to *break off that religious spirit.* You just have to *be radically sold out for Jesus* and *lay it all down*, step out of your comfort zone and *take that leap of faith!*

What Now?

If you're not familiar with the term "*Christianese*," that last statement is a classic example. Words and phrases used in some Christian circles hold fuller meanings than face value. If you speak the language, you know just what each phrase should mean without much explanation. Unfortunately, it can become such a second language, it sometimes sneaks its way in when writing or communicating with others. I try to avoid it, but I decided to include their suggestion because what they are trying to say actually holds some truth.

Funny though, when I heard them explain how easy it is to believe for a dream by first breaking off the religious spirit, I thought to myself, *how ironic*. You see, the use of too much Christianese often indicates a "religious spirit" is present. Part of breaking out of old patterns requires *seeing* them first. Maybe it's not as easy for them as they suggested. But let's look at the truth contained within, despite the irony. What does that statement really mean, practically speaking, when applied to faithfully embracing a dream? Allow me to translate:

- *Break off that religious spirit* = Renounce the lie that following religious traditions and rules make us more righteous or superior to others somehow. Stop thinking our dream is not dream-worthy if it's outside-the-box of religion.

- *Be radically sold out for Jesus* = We have to be willing to put action behind our words, and money where our mouth is.

- *Lay it all down* = Take inventory of our priorities and be willing to rearrange them for the cause.

- *Take that leap of faith* = Courageously do something unfamiliar even if it feels risky, by trusting that God is for you and is in it with you.

Simple small steps, bit by bit, can produce amazing results. They may not feel very productive at the time, maybe even counterproductive here and there, but things aren't always as they seem. At times we have to back up to get a running start. Step by step, like cutting out a paper snowflake, the big reveal gets closer and closer if you dare to keep dreaming and snipping away at it.

What Now?

I've always loved to make those. My dad showed me, when I was really little, just how to fold and cut the paper. As a science teacher, it was very important to him for each paper snowflake to have six points because all actual snowflakes do. So according to Dad, there is only one right way to make a real paper snowflake. Everything else is just a doily. He showed me how to fold and cut any piece of paper into a square, then into a circle; which you then folded in half and then into thirds; one last fold into a skinny wedge shape and you were ready to cut out chunks from all sides to your heart's content. I've made hundreds of decorative cutouts over the years for all kinds of occasions. I never get sick of it. But it's even more special when I can share the art-of-it with another generation of young snowflake-creators. It's the joy of watching their faces as they unfold what appears to be just a creased paper filled with random cuts and snips; their eyes widen as a delicate design emerges before them like a blossoming flower — a unique, six-pointed, unexpected wintry bit of lace. Inevitably, a first-time paper snowflake-maker will immediately want to cut out another. The cutting part isn't what draws them back in. It's the unfolding — the revealing.

As much of a mess as all the snipped away paper scraps make, it's the "negative spaces" they leave behind that make the snowflake so positively delicate and festive. Life feels like a lot of messy negative spaces right now. What do you say we sweep up any of yesterday's negative scraps and just throw them in the air like party confetti? Seeing the positive and fighting to sift through the hype and propaganda to get to

Can you think of any man-made rules that interfered with your once-upon-a-time dream?

the created design hidden beneath the mess, requires "being sure of what you hope for and certain of what you do not see." To get from hype to hope, it takes faith, and real faith takes action. So, let's step on top of past expectations, and step over the fear of disappointment. Dismiss all the man-made rules of what's possible, politically correct, or socially acceptable, and be brave enough to unfold our snowflakes with the sweet expectancy of hope again. It's time to trust in God's genuine, authentic, organic, and real purposes and dreams for us. He's doing a new thing. Now it springs up. Do you not perceive it? If our God can take a man-made pandemic and turn it into a catalyst for making a way in the desert of deferred hope, and streams in the wasteland of broken dreams, then anything is possible, including restoring us to better than new — with dreams intact. Our time for imagining the best, dreaming big, and hoping only in the truth of God's faith-filled Word, has come.

For everything that was written in the past was written to teach us, so that through endurance and the encouragement of the Scriptures we might have hope … May the God of hope fill you with all joy and peace as you trust in him, so that you may overflow with hope by the power of the Holy Spirit. [6]

---

[6] Romans 15:4,13

2:

From What Now to What's New

Do you want to see what kind of frame of mind you are in? You can probably tell by playing a little word association. Here we go:

1. When you hear the question "What now?" which phrase do you add before it in your mind? A.) "Oh no!" or B.) "Okay."

2. You can do pretty much the same with "What's new?" Detect your half-empty or half-full attitude by how you interpret the question. Is it a positive A.) "What's new with you?" or more of a negative B.) "So *what* else is new?"

What Now?

I've experienced both the confusion and anticipation when asking either of those questions, and I have asked them both ways many times. The two books I previously published partly reflected my journey of getting knocked down, getting back up and trying to move on. I found myself looking to God chapter by chapter without a clue asking Him, "Okay, now what?" I didn't know where He wanted to take me next in the book, never mind where He was trying to take me next in my life. Here I am in Book 3, Chapter 2, asking the same questions. I'm still hoping to discover new insight and the new thing that He's doing. What's new? It appears I'm not the only one asking. It seems as if the whole nation is crying out the same two questions at the moment: Oh no! What now? Another crisis. Ugh, so what else is new?

I began writing this chapter in the year 2020. It was a significant year for the whole world because of the pandemic, but a monumental year for the United States because of a series of events spawned by a presidential election, deceitful media, and a government filled with corruption and injustice. It's hard to believe I'm describing "the land of the free and the home of the brave," but seeming even more unreal is what I'm about to convey. The unrest we were experiencing during this unprecedented time of lockdowns, job loss, and uncalled-for mandates, gave rioters of a Marxist movement the flimsy excuse to storm into town squares and even the capitol itself, toppling over statues and defacing monuments of American historical significance. The rebels' all-out fury and claims that this nation was founded on the pure evil of slavery and the inequality of a caste system, made me start questioning my understanding of this nation's identity and God's intent for us.

Then something unexpected rose up within me as I watched the replays of ireful protesters, and my own soul protested: *Oh, wait! They're the ones who are mistaken. They've been so terribly deceived!*

Is the world trying to convince you of something? Have you asked God what He thinks?

What Now?

With the unreliability of mainstream news, and so much social-media censoring, truth is challenging to find these days. So I went to the Author of Truth and asked God what He thought about it all. This is what He said to me:

My Heart is crying for your nation. O, America, how I long to gather you under My wings, just like Jesus, My Son, wept over Jerusalem and longed to gather her like a hen gathers her chicks. This historic moment that is upon you, I foreknew. I have raised this nation up for a time such as this. I planted these United States to be here as a protective Arm for My chosen people, Israel.

The enemy is trying to take it down with its fire and smokescreens. The fires of unrest you are witnessing, I'm allowing to be fanned into a refiner's fire; not to refine the enemy's camp, but to ignite my people who have humbled themselves and turned from their complacency and unbelief; those who have started to cry out to Me on behalf of their nation. The fires will then turn and consume the deadwood and dross of evil.

2: From What Now? to What's New?

Wake up O, Reader of this decree! I'm crying out to you, My loved one, My brave soldier. You have watched. You have prayed and you have listened to so many voices. Confusion, unrest, and the whirlwinds of disruption to your way of life, have made the ground beneath you feel like a row boat on the ocean. I will rescue you.

Look past the waves and find My Son reaching out to you and inviting you to join Him right in the middle of it all. Can you see Him? Do you hear Him? "Come to Me," He says. Lock eyes and feel the fire of His love for you. That's My love flowing together through Him, to you and to your nation. And though it's against all logic to stand up in a boat if you're trying to stay dry, it's pouring buckets and you're already soaking wet — Stand up! Now step out. Defy the gravity of it all, and come to Me.

His words have humbled me to pray and forgive those who have no hope and in hatred and fear are lashing out. Some know exactly what they're doing. Others have fooled themselves into believing their actions are justified, totally persuaded that their motives are pure. I find myself weeping over them, and over the pure insanity and senseless depravity of it all.

Though, I confess there is something else that is also grieving me as I watch the desecration of statues and monuments. It may well be of lesser importance to most, but it is affecting me just the same. As an artist, I find myself empathetically grieving on behalf of the long-since-past artisans who crafted and toiled to create each special memorial; works of art that now lay completely disrespected and defaced. The real value of a statue or monument is given to it by the fame of its creator, what it represents, and its ability to endure through time.

When a statue or marker holds a memory, teaches a lesson, tells a story, or perpetuates an epic life adventure, it turns from being valuable to invaluable. I also felt for the contributors of generations ago who sacrificed and donated whatever they could, whatever it took, to commission each monument's completion so that others would understand the life-changing victory, defeat, or pivotal moment in history that each subject depicted. The hypocrisy displayed by today's misguided tyrants, proves that their selfish tantrum (ignorantly desecrating the very foundation of freedom that allows them such an outburst) is only digging them a deeper hole in which to inevitably fall.

There is such a rich, but often times overlooked, significance in the connections to past generations. I have always felt compelled when passing by old cemeteries to stop and stroll through the rows of names, dates, and epitaphs, pausing to acknowledge the lives of those who walked this earth before me. Old cemeteries hold a special place for me because it's unlikely that too many friends or loved ones are still around to remember or pay tribute to the lives represented there. Sometimes only moss-covered markers with worn-out etchings memorialize lives that profoundly impacted this world, if only for a short season. So many of them infants and toddlers, here for but a breath, just a second in time, and yet their lives (and loss of them) impacted their families in ways we will never understand. The thread that connects me to them all is not just my own mortality, but the ripple effect that one life can have.

What Now?

It's like George Bailey (in the movie *It's a Wonderful Life*) starting to understand how much of a difference his very existence, and even his small acts of kindness along the way, meant to thousands of people and generations who would follow. I reflect on the possible impact each life lived may have had, and ponder the probability that I may not have even been here if it were not for the choices made by those before me. I know it may not fit into the theology and framework of predestination and/or our combined divine destinies, but still I like to take the time to pay tribute and know that one life can affect so many without ever knowing them.

Was there someone in your life who made a real impact, but you never had a chance to tell them? What would you say to them now?

2: From What Now? to What's New?

Yet beyond the connection with a person I never knew, as I read the marker or gravestone, I think about the hands who skillfully and meticulously carved the stone at the tearful request of heartbroken loved-ones grieving a tragic loss. They came to this stonecutter with a hope to memorialize a dearly important life. They come holding purposefully chosen words to help some future reader truly understand how much this person really mattered; that their beloved one made a difference in this world. I think we all at times wonder how our own epitaph will read. For what will we be remembered most? What will our heritage be? Somewhere along the way we have gotten it into our thinking that our dream or life's purpose has to be profoundly dynamic and famously newsworthy; it has to be recognized by

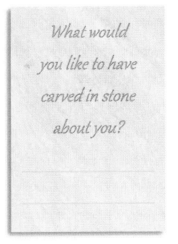

What would you like to have carved in stone about you?

hundreds, if not thousands, of people or followers, in order for it to be counted as a lifetime achievement or considered as our legacy. God is showing me just how far from His heart that mistaken idea really lies.

Walking through a cemetery may sound a bit morbid to you, so let's talk about Christmas instead. Isn't it interesting how a Christmas ornament can connect you to not just memories of your own Christmas' past, but to an entirely different generation of Christmases? We inherited a number of heirloom ornaments that annually donned my grandparents' trees for over 60 years. Some are so dated and worn; some beautifully handmade, but all are irreplaceable. To me they've become invaluable. There's something unique about the connections we have to those who have gone before us that enriches the present like nothing else.

The recent fascination of millions of curious people taking advantage of ancestry-tracing websites, clues me in that I'm probably not alone in my opinion. There are things besides DNA that connect a part of us to the pioneers who blazed the family trail on which we find ourselves walking. Traditions, stories, songs, photographs, and even pieces of clothing, can heighten our awareness of what a legacy truly can mean.

2: From What Now? to What's New?

Some families' unsung heroes were brave enough to forge new trails off the beaten path by breathing new life into old patterns or ways of thinking. Can I be so brave as to entertain the thought that I, too, can blaze a trail?

I might just have enough rebel in me to pull it off. I have been known to break a few traditions here and there; like nixing adult family gift-exchanges at Christmas and creating our own post-Christmas family holiday in January when everything in the world is 80% off and all the stress of deadlines has passed. The matriarchs (my sister Cynthia and I) buy everyone socks, "wrap" them all in brown lunch bags, pass them out randomly and then have a "Sock Swap" till you can trade for the socks you really want. Easy, fun, stress-free and who doesn't love getting a new pair of socks?

I'm sure we have all had a Christmas wish at one time or another. It probably didn't involve socks, but I would hope at least one of your really important wishes actually came true for you. I wonder if the generations of dreamers and wish-makers before me, felt as if they had accomplished their purpose or mission before leaving for the other side of eternity. Did they even have a God-given dream or an idea of their life's purpose? Were they famous or popular? Did their lives impact hundreds of people? What if me being born generations later was their main reason for being here on this planet? What if I'm actually an answer to someone's bedtime "God, bless So-and-so" prayers. What if you are?

Pop quiz time! Is everybody ready? Get out your #2 pencils and list numbers 1-12.

There are 12 very famous people who have been memorialized for all time by having their names listed together in the world's most published and read book —
The Holy Bible.

Name:

28

They are often referred to as The Twelve, and most "church folk" will have an idea of who you're referring to if they hear the term. Just to clarify, I'm not talking about the sons of Jacob. I'm referring to the 12 original apostles (or "sent ones"). But how many of them can you name? Go ahead now and try, before you read any further.

Even people who don't read the Bible much have probably heard of Peter (aka: Simon-Peter), Judas Iscariot and maybe doubting Thomas. Some might be tempted to guess Luke, Mark or even Paul (sorry, Biblical yes, part of The Twelve, no). If you *are* pretty familiar with the New Testament, most likely you are able to name Andrew, James, John, and Matthew. "Bartholomew" was a kick to say when I was a child trying to memorize the apostles' names, but he was also referred to as Nathanael (which confusingly made 13 apostles when counting on your fingers trying to recite them). Let's not forget Philip. He and Nathanael were good friends even before they met Jesus. But the three least-likely names to make their way onto your list, and probably because they would have to surprisingly be on it twice, are: the other Judas who they called Thaddeus, a second James (son of Alphaeus), and another Simon called "the Zealot."

How did you do? If you're like me, half of the spaces on your list were blank or filled with creative guesses. Evidently, memorizing them as a child did not stick very well with me. And yet these very important people were hand-picked and commissioned by Jesus Himself to represent Him. They were chosen by God to begin a revolution meant to reproduce His Kingdom here on earth. They were dearly important to Jesus. Like monuments, the fame of their Creator gave them value. Their names and what they stood for have endured millennia. Following Jesus so closely marked them as permanently as engraved granite witnessing to generations. Their story may be summed up in only a name or a few sentences but even so, their lives were heroic! I wonder what *their* epitaphs read. The fact is that these outcasts of bottom-rung social servants, were chosen by their Creator and He relabeled them "His friends." Isn't it odd that we know so little about them? They are, nonetheless, invaluable.

2: From What Now? to What's New?

There was also a group of 72 courageous others sent out by Jesus, as well as a radical group of 120 believers who waited patiently and obediently in the upper room at Pentecost for God's Holy Spirit to empower them. They all had names, but most were not recorded down for us to know. Their missions were groundbreaking, but all we know about the majority of them is the number of people in their group. Mind you, their group's number is recorded not just in *any* book, or on some man-made monument; these groups of nameless "extras" in God's story are so extremely important to the Author and Perfector of our faith, that He mentions them in *His* Book. He counted them invaluable. We may not know or remember their names. But all that really matters is that God absolutely does.

Now this is what the Lord says ... "Do not fear, for I have redeemed you; I have summoned you by name; you are Mine. When you pass through the waters, I will be with you; and when you pass through the rivers, they will not sweep over you. When you walk through the fire, you will not be burned;

the flames will not set you ablaze. For I am the Lord your God, the Holy One of Israel, your Savior..."[7]

God continued by speaking the following to me, and I believe it's for you as well:

As bold as a fire, as sure as dry wood burning
  and smoke rising, but as miraculous as passing through
    the flames unscathed — so is your life before Me.
      Trauma is a flame that cannot hurt you
        when I'm in it with you.

Walk boldly. I'll give you directions like a GPS,
just before you need them. That way you won't jump ahead
and take a turn before it's time. I promise to bring you to
completion — to your destiny.
 I've kept you thus far. I won't stop now.
  You have defied death more times than you know.
    My plans for you cannot be stopped.
      Delayed perhaps, but not stopped.

A defining moment
is about to blow through your world:

---

[7]From Isaiah 43:1-3a

2: From What Now? to What's New?

Change. Separation. Rising Above.
Flying into new dimensions of miracles
and multiplication. Above all else: Trust Me.

The stage is being set. The cast of characters awaits you.
You are the director, but this time I Am the Author!
The dreams and purposes I've had for you since the curtain
went up, the ones you were born and trained to thrive in,
are waiting just in front of you.

So keep living and loving, but please, start walking.
Your destiny is just one hill away.
Not a mountain... a hill.

What now? He wants to heal us now so we can confidently, and expectantly move ahead into what's new — possibly an old, forgotten dream reborn. His best for us has always been available. We just have to be ready, willing, and daring enough to say,

"Okay, what now, God? What's new?"

What Now?

Was there something God said to me, that was also for you?

_____

_____

_____

_____

_____

_____

_____

_____

3:

From Fright to Flight

Will we ever be brave enough to dream again? Jesus says, "With God, all things are possible."[8] It appears as if He might be trying to wake up some doubting and discouraged dreamers around here. He has His dream for each of us, and an entire plan beginning to end of how to accomplish it. Our grandest of revelatory ideas are just droplets in the ocean compared to what He has for us. We stand holding a big old seashell to our ear hoping to at least hear the ocean's echo. He longs to offer us the whole ocean of His vast wisdom, but understands we are not that absorbent. Lovingly,

---

[8] Matthew 19:26

What Now?

He bends down to whisper His ideas for us, hoping we'll be able to at least grasp *some* inspiration, enough this time, to put down the conch and finally jump in with both feet.

"Inspiration" sounds so happy and lighthearted, doesn't it? But don't let it fool you. True inspiration, when planted in a heart by God's Holy Spirit, is often met with mental interference, resistance, and voices of discouragement (like not so hypothetically finding out, while struggling through writing the first chapter of a book you thought you heard God tell you to write, that a well-known preacher/author is about to publish a book on the same topic). What is intended to be "stepping into a beautiful thing" can quickly turn into an ugly wrestling match of dragging heels and stubborn excuses: But I don't really have the time right now, God. I don't really feel like it at the moment. Besides, I have nothing to say and somebody else already wrote a book about this. It's as if God said back to me:

Really? And who are you to pick and choose if you have spare time to give away when only I know how much time I've given you to accomplish what you're created to do? What makes you think the precious time that I've given you is to be spent only on behalf of yourself, doing things the easiest most pain-free way possible, or only when "you feel like it" and if it's convenient?

And, you know that other author? He needed to learn something by writing his book. I have something for you to learn while writing this one. Don't be afraid. Just listen and get to it.

I have a plan to reveal My heart if you reveal yours. You know I already see it, but do you? No more rationalizing or making excuses. Trust Me and take courage!

God knows there's fear trying to hide behind my excuses, and that I need to be reminded to take courage. I know firsthand that if we have been betrayed or rejected by someone in authority who we trusted, it can cause after-effects of fear and rebellion to set in (as deflectors and self-protectors). And obviously, that can be the cause of the conflict and apprehension we feel when God's voice of authority is nudging us toward His dream for us. Even though deep down that dream is our true desire, fear and rebellion find reasons to say "no." Finding excuses to back away from making our dreams come true becomes our go-to preservation technique. Excuses like: Well, everyone comes up with creative ideas and wishful thoughts now and again. How do I even know if what I'm dreaming about is from God?

Actually, that's a good question: How *can* we tell if a dream or desire is truly God inspired? One way is that His dreams for us can only be accomplished by working alongside Him. If it's from Him it will demand abilities and resources we just don't have on our own. If we did, it would be more of a goal and not so much of a dream. Reach a goal and we feel accomplished. Realize a dream, and *God* gets all the credit and glory. We were made to bring glory and joy to our Creator. He made each of us for His good pleasure and His amazing purposes.[9] He plants eternity in our

What are some of your best excuses?

_____

_____

_____

_____

---

[9] See Philippians 2:13

hearts and gives us dreams and visions.[10] Dreaming with Him is meant to be exciting; not only for us, but exciting for God as well!

Maybe that's why the devil tries so hard to discourage us from dreaming and why we find ourselves giving up before we even start. Believing his lie that "you can make all your dreams come true if you only set your mind to it" can leave the dreamer in us completely disillusioned and feeling very inadequate, especially if after many attempts, our dream has not manifested. Regrets, guilt, or shame over past traumatic failures can make us feel unworthy of ever trying again. We end up escorting our heart's desire out the side door as soon as it tries to take a seat in our imaginations.

But when we do surrender to God — our loving, kind, inspiration Giver who's only trying to share something with us so we can share it with the world — obeying Him has a way of gratifying a piece of our souls that otherwise just turns to rebellious frustration. There are occasions I'm sure we've all experienced

---

[10] See Ecclesiastes 3:11 and Acts 2:17

when God's dream has called us to attention, but our at-ease frame of mind snubbed its nose at Him, pretending to be disinterested. More than likely though, what we heard Him telling us to do sounded too risky, too impossible, way outside our comfort zone. That's the real reason we stood there humming "la-la-la" with our ears blocked, hoping His assignment would sound less scary when muffled. Unfortunately, sounding "risky" is another indication that a dream really *is* from Him.

Proverbs 13:12 begins: "Hope deferred makes the heart sick..." More than likely we have played a big part in some of our own hope being deferred. Here's a few probable ways we can become our own dream crushers without even trying:

- If we nervously talk ourselves out of taking action while listening to naysayers and dream critics, we become accomplices.

- We dwell on the times that God allowed us to walk into difficult places where we experienced frustration, failure, and painful circumstances. It was our choice, our bright idea to go, and He only allowed it to show us where we were lacking and how much we truly need Him, but now we're blaming Him for not preventing us from going. We say we're "finding it hard to trust Him" when in reality, we're simply too busy pouting to listen.

- We self-sabotage when we determine God's preparation time (meant to ready us for His blessing) is taking way too long, and we give up on it, shrugging, "Guess it wasn't from God."

The first step to remedy the effects of abandoned dreams, is to humbly brush the disappointment off our prayer-worn knees, knock the chip of prideful impatience off our shoulders, and take an honest look back at that last time when things didn't work out so well; honest enough to think that perhaps the previous failed attempt may not have been so fulfilling even if it *had* succeeded. Was that last dream even from God? Maybe we were only hoping it was Him because it sounded attainable. "I have this great idea, God. Now could You please bless it?" Sound familiar?

How can we tell if a dream is from God? Proverbs 13:12 concludes: "but a longing fulfilled is a tree of life." Dreams from God are going to be full of life, deeply rooted in love, and its fulfillment will always honor Him, and not necessarily us. For the dreamer, they are meant to be exciting, rewarding, and life-changing. They may feel big and scary, but God makes sure it's well worth the venture.

What are you hoping God will ask you to do first?

I know new dreams can remind us of past failures and unanswered wishes, but God is patiently waiting to help us get past our past. When we're ready to try again, He will lower our wounded dreamers' defenses by easing us forward with gentler suggestions. He knows we like pain free and easy, so He'll usually start there. Then like pre-labor practice-contractions, if we hear His voice and respond by taking action, He will give us something else to try, but maybe requiring us to be a little more daring. He builds on our obedience, increases our confidence and the joyful rewards as well. The key is to be faithful in the small things so He can trust us with more.[11] Even the small things don't feel so small in the moment though. Yet God knows just the right amount of tension to apply to sure up our courage. He starts with something we like to do and then ups the ante slightly as we go.

For me, it was writing. I enjoy finding words to express ideas and feelings; fitting them all together and then arranging them to flow. God teaches me so much about life as I write. When I sit and listen for Him, pencil in hand, new ideas flow onto the paper that I never would have thought of on my own. I know they're from God because when I read it back to myself it actually surprises me. Even knowing how writing benefits me, and the joy that it usually brings me, getting me to sit down and write something significant takes a real nudge — more like a shove.

God starts it like butterflies somewhere in my spirit and if I don't reach for a pencil and paper, the butterflies start sounding like mosquitoes. I can swat them away and ignore the inspiration or give in and write. You may not be a writer, but whatever your

---

[11] See Luke 16:10

passion and gifts are indicating God's intent is for you to do, sweet relief is hiding within you if you're willing to follow His lead, take action, speak up, take a chance, and let those butterflies flutter into the atmosphere. Has God inspired you yet? Might you be ignoring the butterflies? If so, I totally get it.

When God prompted me to write my first book (*Get Back on the Horse? GOD, You Can't Be Serious!*), I had nearly forgotten what a dream was made of, never mind entertain the idea of creating something new with God. It had been so long since I'd let myself go there. I was burned out from life, ministry, caregiving, and some major losses. God had to confirm to me that it really was Him suggesting it. At that point in my life, convincing me to even *try* to write again took Him using some very clear, personally specific ways. But He is so gentle and kind, and He made it so evident that writing the book was part of His storyline and healing therapy for me, that six months later the rough draft was complete. Then it was time to edit and publish it. That was a different story altogether.

3: From Fright to Flight

The hesitation and fear were palpable. I didn't think I could handle having people criticize or reject my "new baby." Add to that not having even a clue of the logistics of self-publishing, and a nearly completed manuscript was kept safely in a drawer, collecting dust for well over a year. Fear of rejection and feelings of inadequacy had paralyzed me. Even though God graciously assured me waiting was okay because He was working behind the scenes to set me up to be ready to move forward, I would still hear the haunting sound of war drums vibrating from the drawer each time I passed it. The steady beat of guilt would gnaw at me as it crescendoed: *finish what you started ... finish what you started ... finish now, finish now ... finish, finish, FINISH!* I had been a project starter for a good part of my life and had to work hard at learning to complete whatever I began. The pendulum may have swung a mite too far.

I had never written a book before, and doing anything for the first time can make us feel awkwardly unsure of ourselves. Turned out the writing part of the book wasn't the hardest part. It was the unfamiliar publishing process and all the "what ifs" that scared me the most. I can see you shaking your head right now thinking *this woman is such a wimp!* I realize you've probably faced life issues and much riskier assignments far worthier of fear, but maybe the principle of overcoming them all, will be the same.

Facing the fear of whatever roars at you, begins by discerning the lie behind it. Even things with a kitteny "mew" that make you feel uneasy enough to try to avoid them, need to be faced at some point. The bottom line is that fear indicates we've been duped into thinking that something, or someone, is bigger and more powerful than the omnipotent God of the Universe. Consider how absurd it is to think that our Heavenly Father (who lovingly watches over and cares deeply about every aspect of our lives from conception to eternity) could possibly be intimidated by anything and somehow not do what's best for us. When we don't believe that God is going to show up and rescue us out of it, or that what concerns us is in some way outside of His jurisdiction, and even though it's way outside of ours, we cope by pretending we can take charge of it — by worrying.

That's really what worrying is: trying to control something we have no control over and mistakenly thinking that if we fret enough, it will make some sort of positive difference. Oh, I know all about fretting. It is something I've practiced a lot. I'm practically a  professional (though I know better). The thing is, I'm the first one to tell you that casting your cares on Jesus, letting Him carry the burden and the brunt of the heavy yoke, will absolutely alleviate the weight on your shoulders and help put life back into balance for you. And it certainly *sounds* simple enough; except how in the world do we cast invisible cares that we can't seem to get a grip on, onto an invisible Rescuer who we don't think we really are worthy to have in the first place? Why attempt something so impracticable?

Is God reminding you of something that you're "taking charge of" again?

What Now?

Other than the fact that we're not designed to carry heavy emotional loads like fear, worry, and anxiety, holding on to them is actually sinful and unhealthy. You may think fear shows lack of faith, but contrary to that common thought, fear is *not* the absence of faith. In fact, its very presence indicates we have lots of faith. We've simply placed it in something we irrationally consider bigger than God. God is the only One, His Sovereignty is the only thing, deserving of fear and trembling. Any other fear object is just an imposter. To fear it is a twisted form of worship. But the main reason we should cast our cares on Jesus is because God tells us to. [12] And God never tells us to do something that isn't important for us, or that He doesn't give us the tools to do.

Speaking the truth of Scripture aloud is effective at overriding fear and combatting the lies behind it. It also addresses the ailments caused by worry and anxiety by working like an analgesic and antioxidant at the same time. The Name of Jesus, the Blood of the Lamb, and the Word of God are a triple threat that

[12] See 1 Peter 5:7

when combined, create an unstoppable Remedy for whatever ails us.

There is a whole Book full of promises and truths we can use to counteract fear-induced physical ailments, emotional torment, and negative ideas. Here are just a few for us to read out loud (written in first person to make them more relatable):

- I have not been given a spirit of fear, but of power, love, and a sound, disciplined mind (see 2 Timothy 1:7).

- I've been given authority by Jesus Himself to trample on snakes and scorpions [demonic forces] and to overcome *all* the power of the enemy; nothing can harm me (see Luke 10:19).

- There is now no condemnation in Christ Jesus, and I am free from any condemning charges made against me (see Romans 8:1, 31-34).

- No weapon formed against me will prosper (see Isaiah 54:17).

- As soon as I confess my sins to Him (agreeing with Him that what I did, or failed to do, was wrong or unhealthy), God is faithful and just to forgive my sins and cleanse me from *all* unrighteousness (see 1 John 1:9).

- In Jesus I've become the righteousness of God and have right standing in His eyes no matter what (see 2 Corinthians 5:21).

Hearing ourselves say the truth out loud, even if we don't believe it right away, shifts something in our brain. Combine that with the truth of God's Word ministering to our spirit, and declarations become a primary force to maintain health, renew minds, and overcome anything! Knowing that the dream Proposer never intended for us to dream without Him, should encourage those of us who may have failed to accomplish past dreams on our own, to try it again, but this time *with* Him.

Has He brought a hopeful dream or idea back to your mind yet? What has God been tugging at your heart to do lately, or better still, what has He been encouraging you towards your whole life? Most likely it was something daunting when He first suggested you consider it. Now that we know He'll be in it with us all the way, it only feels ... okay, it still feels pretty gigantic. We just have to remember God is always bigger.

When we understand that we are only the weak inadequate vessels God has chosen to use to display *His* power, it frees us to not only dream again, but to dream big. He gives us big dreams, not to scare us but to humble us. He incorporates with each a mustard seed of faith and a raindrop of inspiration. How quickly a dream takes root or begins to grow all depends on the condition of the soil — our willingness to cooperate and submit to God's purposes. That means weeding out all fear, and not arguing with the Sower of our destiny. This might be a good time to remember that obedience is meant to be rewarding. By opting out, or maybe arguing with God's idea, we forfeit the sweet promise of reward, and sacrifice the fun of dreaming and creating something amazing with Him. Unfortunately, if we take a pass often enough, we may become hardened to God's voice. With our history of not following through, He may even stop suggesting new possibilities. It's not that He doesn't want to direct our path and make it straight, it's just that we quit acknowledging Him.[13] When inspiration strikes, we need to be able to believe God for the impossible and be quick to obey. Forget what is behind (any failures or entanglements) and press on to what God is calling you toward just ahead.[14] Declaring the truth of His Word, spending time with Him and really listening, then obeying Him with love, is like fluttering your wings — from fright to flight.

There's a fresh start, a clean slate waiting for each of us. The winter iciness of past disappointments and the fear of failure is melting. Do you not perceive it? Sense the warmth of His sunshine and the rose-like fragrance of His approval. Ha, what do you know? Looks like "Sunshine and Roses" are springing up again.

Oh wait, was that a butterfly I just saw fly by?

---

[13] See Proverbs 3:6
[14] See Philippians 3:13-14

4:

From Reel to Real

The first decade of my life was the 1960s. Let's blame my rebellious question-authority tendencies on that, shall we? In fact, let's just blame the whole need for this chapter on that. So much of my sense of reality was formed by a black and white TV screen and its world of canned laughter and perfectly manicured homes filled with perfectly manicured people dressed to the hilt, even at breakfast. Children's weekday programming consisted mostly of clowns, puppets, heroic dogs and horses, and of course a flying man with a cape. My Saturday mornings were delightfully filled by violent cartoon characters with bunny ears, guns, duck feathers, and lots of TNT explosions that blew things to smithereens, yet no one ever got permanently hurt. But as if that wasn't enough, one show that really messed with my reality, was a preschool program with a very nice "teacher" who claimed I was her friend and that she had the ability to see into my living room with her magic mirror. She would end each episode singing her "did all my friends have fun at play" song, and then she'd proceed to look into the camera-lens through her empty mirror frame to name the names of the children she could somehow see who actually had fun. She even knew when it was someone's birthday. How *did* she do that? Seems a bit invasive, wouldn't you say?

The effects of fantasies and visual images can impact a person's psyche profoundly, especially as children. Without proper parental guidance and explanations, TV shows, books, and movies can cause confusion and even emotional trauma. Seeing as my parents were raised on some pretty gruesome fairy tales (becoming desensitized to a lot of things themselves early on) they still managed to filter much of what we saw for the most part. Other than those explosive Saturday morning cartoons; Oh, and let's not forget that classic trio of slapstick, eye-poking, pie-throwing comedic geniuses; and of course the one movie that left me and so many others scared silly of tornadoes and flying monkeys; other than those, they did pretty well by us. I grow more and more grateful that they were aware of my "sensitivities" and sheltered me from a lot of unnecessary exposure to dark things and complicated concepts. They did their best to avoid the confusion that can be caused by parents who use television as an unsupervised babysitter, or some who take advantage of children's imaginations and control their behavior by insisting imaginary characters are real; characters that get slipped deceptively into a child's world. I won't mention any names, but some characters actually sneak in at night while you're sleeping and leave presents under things like trees and pillows. We still had so much fun knowing we were only pretending about them, and none of the mistrust of being lied to. My parents knew that as you get older, faith is challenging enough, never mind having to overcome not knowing what to believe in or who to trust.

What Now?

Because of its daily visual assault of distorted reality and its commercials constantly brain-washing viewers into feeling discontent, the television became more of an influence in homes than any media before it. The invention of the television, which actually found its way into most American living rooms by the time I was born, was more of an invasion into our real world than the reel-to-reel world of motion pictures had ever previously been. Movies had to be paid for and viewed in a theater, outside of home life, and only on occasion; not daily or nightly for free in the comfort of your own living room, like perpetual company that never leaves.

Early on, the quality and special effects of TV programs were poor enough to know that what you were watching wasn't reality. But even so, we were fascinated by it, and often glued to it thinking we were expanding our horizons and keeping more in step with the real world's bigger picture. As primitive as technology was, it was still beyond our understanding, and we found ourselves being lured in by its "magic" even way back then in its infancy.

4: From Reel to Real

Technology for us children of the 1960s consisted of walkie talkies, transistor radios, pull-string talking dolls, train sets, racetracks, record players, plastic ovens that baked bite-sized cakes with a lightbulb, and the piece de resistance: reel-to-reel tape recorders. Everyone had a television (a certain few had color TV sets, and we definitely found excuses to end up at those friends' houses for Saturday morning cartoons), but if you were lucky enough to own a tape recorder, you were the envy of all your friends. Despite the fact that it distorted a person's voice to the degree that it was difficult to distinguish who was actually speaking, the mystery of technology made it captivating, and everyone wanted to play with it and record just about anything: made up songs, pretend news reports and interviews, silly rhymes, and for some unexplainable reason, burps, raspberries, and other completely obnoxious noises.

Like an abstract painting next to a photograph, it was obvious how comparatively "unrealistic" it all was. Nobody complained. We didn't know any better. We were still conditioned from reading books and listening to stories and were able to use our imaginations to forgive the obvious split screens, fill in the gaps, and ignore the cables making the hero fly. Even though it was quite unlike the deception and confusion today's technology can cause, young imaginations were still affected by it.

Most of our present-day mind-boggling technology can be summed up in two words: virtual reality. The distortion of what is naturally real, recreated by unnatural means, produces images and stories along with emotionally provoking surround-sound scores

Was there a mistaken idea you were so sure was true, that even now it's hard to admit it's not?

and special effects that may not actually be happening *to* us in real life, but register in our brains and bodies as if they were. Even if we're sitting at home watching a TV show, remote in our hand to turn it on or off, what we can't shut off is our adrenaline, emotions, and natural instincts that respond involuntarily to whatever we allow our senses to absorb. It's almost impossible to override them. With computer animation as sophisticated and believable as it has become, I often find myself reaching for a box of tissue repeating, "It's just a cartoon ... It's just a cartoon." What really exposes my gullibility, and how easily drawn in I am, is when I catch myself criticizing the probability of the storyline or the motivation of a character and how in real life, they wouldn't say such a thing, and then I realize it's an animated talking fish in question here. How much believable motivation does the fish really need? Black and white film, distorted recordings, and primitive animation are helpful for me to distinguish "reel" from "real" but even so, good acting and happy endings can still tug at my heartstrings.

Maybe it's the downside of not being desensitized at an early age, or maybe it's exactly the way God intended me to be at this point, but here I am, imagining and feeling feelings that aren't always just my own. Connecting with others is part of what we're wired to do, yet we all connect to different degrees and at different levels. I've been very empathetic of other people's emotions since I was a child. Even the feelings of stuffed animals and dolls need to be considered. I bet you didn't know that. As a child, I instinctively knew that they all needed to be able to see and breathe when you put them away on the shelf. And if it was back to their toy box, it only made sense to have to leave the top open a crack. I'd like to think it's the gift of compassion and not some crazy personality quirk, but whatever it is, it seems to take place in my imagination.

Now imagination can be a wonderful thing, except when, even as an adult, you can sense that toys in the clearance bin at the bargain outlet must be feeling rejected and unwanted enough already, and should probably be arranged to make them at least able to see ... um ... I mean at least able to *be* seen by potential buyers. You'll be glad to know I've learned to control my impulses to rearrange while shopping (at least when there are others watching), but can you imagine what happens to me when I see actual children or people abandoned by family or society, and labeled as a clearance item, or worse — discarded. Even when on film or in a storybook, I have to guard my heart from what I take in so that I'll have something left of my heart when required to value and love any real-life people God puts in front of me. The purely secular and negative narrative painted by many authors, entertainers, fictional news, and a censored social media, can send my understanding of reality reeling. When their version of reality collides with my spiritual perception of it, I know it's time to change the channel. What do you do when every station is playing the same program?

It's not always easy, but distinguishing between what is real and what's just fabricated or imaginary is important for dreamers to be able to do. I'm not just talking about the mountains of fictional misinformation we're bombarded with every day, but the giants and mountains in our minds that come in all kinds of forms and sizes. They appear very real as they stand between us and our impossible dream. This in-between realm that we call "Imagination" is often thought of as purely a world of fantasy. But it's so much more than that. Before dreams are born, they are conceptualized here. Beyond being a place where new concepts and creations come into existence, it's our place to meet with God, hear His plans, sense His presence, perceive His Kingdom Realm and dream with Him. Imagine that! It's the place where we ask Him life's questions, get ideas and work out solutions. It's hardly a fantasy. It's all *very* real, it's just not a tangible kind of real.

My need to sort out what appears to be actual reality from the intangibly real eternal truths of a matter, is imperative to conquering what stands before me now (and I'm sensing, maybe before you as well).

Are you presently standing in the shadow of a giant? Do you know its name?

The struggle to see my dream manifest is personal for me. My compassion and desire to see people free from sickness, chronic pain, and mental or emotional torment, has been met with a mountain of resistance and a seemingly giant contradiction. I've experienced mental harassment, lack of confidence, and lifelong physical challenges.

Observe where challenges typically occur in your life, and what it is you tend to struggle with the most, and you'll probably find what your "calling from God" is calling you towards. For example: The fact that I have a back condition most likely caused by a major surgery and radiation treatments as a child, and the fact that the devil tried to take me out early on in life, clues me in that I'm called to help heal others physically and emotionally. God's Holy Spirit has empowered me with gifts of discernment, counseling, and prophetic insight. Life has also taught me a few helpful things along the way, medically and emotionally speaking. I've experienced some very dark demonic encounters due to the fear left behind by the medical trauma, as well as typical childhood fears. The encounters themselves fed into everyday anxiety, fear of pain, and an unhealthy fear of satan.

Fear is a weapon used by demonic forces to open doors into our minds and emotions. Deliverance from fears and the lies behind them closes those doors. God taught me the truth of my authority over demonic influence and negativity. It's the authority that every believer has when Jesus lives within them, and I am passionate about sharing with others the freedom and power we're meant to experience.

God miraculously healed me from cancer, and I know He wants me to experience complete healing from the back condition it caused. He proved it by intervening some years ago and I had pain-free mobility for a good long while, and then for whatever reason… it returned. While operating in the gifts of healing and deliverance for years now, we have come to see that when physical healing or freedom from trauma are not tangibly evident even after much prayer and declaration, or when an ailment returns, there is often a spiritual/emotional underlying reason for it.[15] I have looked for "open doors." I've taken spiritual inventory: is there fear, unforgiveness, or habitual sin? Are there generational patterns or ungodly alliances? Those things can give permission for afflictions to stick

---

[15] For some examples in Scripture see Luke 13:10-16, Matthew 8:16-17 & 9:2-7

around or come back. I've personally wrestled with it many times, done serious soul searching, received wise counsel, but the pain still lingers. Physical limitations are challenging the dream; even my sitting here to write this now is uncomfortable for me, never mind the physical demands of what I feel God is about to have me do in this next season of life. This was my prayer I wrote to Him just today:

Father God,

You are so beyond my imagination, but I know this is where my spirit sees the Kingdom. It's such a battle to block out the interferences and distractions. It's like I'm trying to erase any preconceived ideas of what to expect, so I can have more room and a clear path to experience and envision what You really have for me. Is there something in me blocking the path, or could it be I'm just afraid of what You might show me? Am I not trusting You again? You promised me that You "have my back" and I knew it was You speaking to me through that prophet. It brings me such joy to think my back is really being healed.

Okay ... so, um ... I confess that I may have slightly, well more than slightly, doubted You? Oh God, I really doubted

What Now?

You. I'm sorry. Please forgive me. I'm sorry that You've had to continually encourage me to keep believing, keep dreaming, keep trusting. You say I'm healed. You never lie.

So what's my deal? It's just that the physical symptoms and pain keep shouting otherwise — and quite loudly I might add. God, I know that in Your presence, there is healing. Boldly I come in to the Holy of Holies accessible to me through the torn Veil — the Broken Body of Jesus — because You've invited me here. So here I am. What's holding me back from experiencing the reality of my physical healing right now? Is it fear of change? Maybe I'm just too used to being this way; too used to excusing myself from physically demanding assignments. Am I addicted to the sympathy?

Maybe my physical challenges are an indication of spiritual challenges that still need conquering first. Is the pain in my back a visible outward reflection of something that You are addressing on the inside of me? Do I need "more backbone"? Am I overwhelmed by something (Oh, my aching back)?

Here I am again wondering is this really part of my destiny — living with this chronic annoyance? Is this part of the destination You've prepared for me, and prepared me for? What's Your dream for me, God? How do You see me? I can't imagine it includes these physical limitations.

Okay ... Alright ... I surrender. You are the Living God. With you ALL things are possible. The fact that I'm still alive is living proof of that.

My real prayer is that the rest of my days will reflect the glory and reality of Your undeniable healing power, and that I will be a living testament of the power You give us to see others healed and whole! I trust in You and in the power of Jesus' Name. Thank You for whatever it is You have for me ... Amen.

What do we do when we've seen faith work for so many others and even in our own life before, but now this giant of a mountain just won't budge? I've come to the conclusion that this must be God's ultimate resistance training. Unanswered prayer is a unique opportunity to fortify our faith by truly believing without seeing and being certain of what we hope for. It takes knowing that we know (*really* know) that our God is forever faithful; so much so, our certainty becomes unshakable.

What Now?

Whatever it is, whatever God has planned, obviously will take enormous amounts of faith on our part. If our faith has needed this much testing and strengthening in order to meet the amazing challenges ahead, I can only imagine the dream assignments we are about to walk into, the incredible miracles, signs and wonders we are about to experience, and all the exciting prayers we're going to see God answer (practically before we get done praying them).

All healing is a gift to us from God, but I believe supernatural healing that cannot be scientifically explained away, is what gives Him the most glory. Waiting for it builds faith, and faith pleases God. I must admit that up to this point, I have been waiting for God to make the next move. When in actuality, I think now He's waiting for me. He is waiting for me to grab hold of His promise that I am *already* healed. As my faith strengthens, my grip on reality becomes

What is it that's bothering you the most but could actually be making your faith stronger?

stronger too. All who have prayed for me, and believed with me over the years, will be part of the celebration when the healing Jesus made possible so long ago, is finally revealed and manifested in my physical body.

In the meantime, writing this all out has brought me to a place of peace, so thank you for going here with me for the moment. It has given me a slightly different perspective of reality that I'd like to share with you in hopes that it might help you, too:

King Jesus,

I stand on top of Your absolute victory over death, disease, and infirmities. I stand perched high above on this Rock-solid mountaintop to have a clear view of my position in You, and the complete advantage that You have gained for me. I stand behind the Shield of Blood that skews the enemy's view of me, and I roar the Name of Jesus with You, as Your roar shakes my adversaries to their very core.

I am more than a conqueror in You because I have the victory before I even begin to fight. But by fighting, by using my voice and engaging my spirit, I strengthen my faith and I get to enjoy the power and authority You have bestowed upon me. I get to watch symptoms leave, all harassment and interference cease, and miracles happen in front of my eyes. Nothing can compare to the joy of answered prayer and watching tormenting demons flee at the sound of Your Name.

The only greater joy is knowing that my name is forever written in Your Book of Life. I get to know You and hug You (even though you are King) and weep tears of joy and adoration at Your feet, and to worship Your awesomeness forever. I get to witness You and our Father and Holy Spirit, in all Your glory and mystery, abiding and interacting; stepping in and out of One Another in perfect unity. I can only imagine it for now.

But knowing my future with You is based on Your victory and grace, raises me up to a vantage point of certainty and assurance that no weapon formed against me will prosper!

Amen!

Have you been trusting God to fulfill a long-awaited promise or maybe to finally answer that hopeful whispered prayer? What dream have you tucked away because it has looked more and more impossible as time passes? Maybe you've convinced yourself that you must have misheard God or just come up with that crazy dream on your own; maybe it was just wishful thinking — just your imagination. Go there with God for a minute. Step into your imagination with Him. Bring the vision of the dream with you. He'll let you know if He planted it in you or not. Let Him show you what it would look like completed, and then let Him deepen your desire to see it happen.

When a dream is from God, the truth of it will ring louder and longer than any flimsy practical-side objections. And isn't it true that even a  total fantasy seen on the big screen can impact our spirits when the truth of bravery and sacrificial love are at the heart of the story? When that impossible dream you have imagined for so long is given to you by God, it will echo even stronger and deeper in your heart than the most epic of all epic reel-to-reel adventures.

What movie would best depict the challenge you're facing and the victory that's just ahead?

What Now?

No, I can't see through a TV camera lens by peering with an empty, handheld mirror-frame to know if you had fun at play. But I do know an all-powerful God who knows and loves you, and sees the *real* you, no magic mirror required. He really does want us to have fun and enjoy life to the full by getting to know Him and getting to love Him back. He wants to give us the desires of our heart as we delight in Him[16] by enjoying His company, laughing with Him, and receiving His love. And *His* love is a dream come true...

And as real as reality will ever get!

---

[16] Psalm 37:4

5:

From Waiting to Wanting

A package is about to arrive today. It's been about 10 days in the waiting, and that feels like forever to a child who used his birthday money to purchase the most "awesomenest" thing *ever!*" Even though the tracking app assures us it will be today, history has shown that "arrives by" times can quickly turn into "delivery delayed" at any given moment. Cautious optimism builds despite the possibility of disappointment.

Whether it's waiting for the words to flow onto the first page of a chapter about waiting to wanting, or for the purchase of a youngster's lifetime to finally arrive in the mail, or waiting for the tea kettle to boil so I'll have something to warm my hands and calm my nerves while we wait (inadvertently proving the phenomenon that a watched pot never boils); waiting is not something we generally like to do. Waiting of any kind translates into perseverance (even writing that 12-letter word takes stamina). But persevere we will! What other choice do we have?

Being persistent in an endeavor until results happen, inspired the early 17th century proverb: All things come to those who wait. Abraham Lincoln added "…to those who wait, but only the things left by those who hustle." Woodrow T. Wilson quipped, "All things come to him who waits — provided he knows what he's waiting for." And like nick names come to those who wait with long hard-to-pronounce names, over time the phrase became simply: All things in time.

I had always heard that proverb quoted as: "*Good* things come to those who wait." If I have to be patient (patience *is* a virtue), I'd much rather be waiting for something good. Have you noticed how your endurance level and emotional response can be affected by what it is you're waiting for, and if it's your choice to wait or not? Think about the following scenarios and imagine how differently you might feel for each:

If you were waiting…

.. for Christmas morning.

.. for Christmas morning, with an engagement ring in your pocket.

.. for a chatty phone caller to hang up.

.. for a prom date to finally call.

Now pay attention to how your body reacts as you imagine waiting…

.. in line at the DMV with your impulsive teenager.

.. in line for the midnight premier showing of the best blockbuster movie series finale ever created!

.. in the crowded ER with a sick child.

.. in the dugout of a crowded stadium, next at bat, when your team is down by one run, last inning, 2 outs, 1 runner on base, the batter is 3 and 2, and this game decides the championship.

What Now?

Notice anything? Waiting is definitely something that can produce a physical response (usually felt in our gut or shoulders) even when we're only imagining the wait. Emotionally, it can stir up a desire in us that we didn't even know was there. Waiting can easily expose a wanting or a longing we often describe as heartache. It isn't really absence itself that makes the heart grow fonder. It's more the length of the absence that does. There must be something to it because that saying has been around for a very long time. It was the first line of an anonymous love poem initially published in 1602.

What songs or poems about "longing" come to your mind?

Missing loved ones and missing home are inherent. And it seems the longer the wait the stronger the want becomes.

The truth and pain of longing has carried its way into countless sayings, lyrics and poetry. I'm sure you can think of at least a few love songs about missing someone, wanting them back, or waiting for their answer, where vows containing words like "always" and "forever" or desperately outrageous promises are strongly declared. Norman Gimbel wrote:

> *If it takes forever, I will wait for you.*
> *For a thousand summers, I will wait for you.*

Forever? You really think so, Norman? Maybe for one summer. But a thousand? I guess when love is on the line, our distorted perception of time and over-estimation of our tolerance level become painfully apparent, especially when set to music.

Waiting is just a part of life I suppose. I can't think of any fun kind of waiting. Can you? There's really nothing enjoyable about minutes that feel like hours, or years that turn into decades. Perhaps, what we do while we're waiting can help to pass the time and make waiting a bit more tolerable. But even the best guessing games or good reading books don't bring the same kind of usual joy if they're done while waiting. Is there anything worth waiting for, that actually makes the wait worth it?

What Now?

There must be something good for us about biding our time, because God has made it an ongoing part of the human experience. All through Scripture the most impactful God-appointed leaders found themselves waiting and wondering for long periods of time for their hopes and dreams to manifest.

Jesus' followers and friends who experienced His physical presence and got to love Him in person, had waited their whole lives for the Messiah to rescue them, as had all of mankind back to Adam and Eve. The twelve young men Jesus chose to specifically train for leadership (and some for martyrdom), were so young they had not waited long, but the tragedy they would endure matured them quickly. They had grown to love and cherish their Teacher/Messiah who called them friends. They were waiting to see God's Kingdom come to Israel. They knew that they all held a special place in Jesus' heart and in His coming government because He had specifically chosen them. They had experienced His perfect love and now they would have to experience not only the devastation and grief of seeing Him crucified, but having their dreams and expectations — everything they sacrificed three years believing for — crushed, lost, and obliterated before their eyes. Now they feared for their own lives. Add to their grief that their Friend's grave was then supposedly robbed, and all their waiting and wanting had come to nothing. Or had it?

Three days later the resurrected, fully alive, conquering King Jesus returned to them. They took 40 days and caught their breath; regaining their hope listening to Jesus teach about the Kingdom and getting their last-minute instructions. When they got brave enough and asked Him when His Kingdom would finally manifest on earth, He basically said it wasn't for them to know. They would just have to wait and see. He told them to go to Jerusalem and wait for the gift of the Holy Spirit promised to them by His Father. More waiting? Was this a test? Was He just kidding around? And then what did the angels tell them as they stood dumbfounded staring into the sky after He left their sight by ascending into the clouds? Essentially, "He's coming back. You'll see." Which in essence meant more waiting.

What Now?

Clearly God knows that something significant happens in the "abiding" times. When you trust someone who has a good track record and they tell you that something you really want is on the way, you pretty much live your life as if you already have it, don't you? You don't usually fret that it won't ever arrive. What about when the Lord of everything, Who is completely sovereign and perfectly trustworthy, promises you something (or Someone) is coming to you but the arrival time is meant to be a surprise? What if the time you were hoping for and that made the most sense to you, comes and goes, but no surprise (except the surprise that it didn't come)? Do you start looking forward to the new arrival time, or choose not to, for fear of being disappointed again?

The Bible could logically be retitled *Just Wait.* It is the theme of so many chapters with pages full of adjectives like long-awaited, long-suffering, and "How long O, Lord?" Think of the millions of other names and stories of blessed people and instant miracles that could have been included in a Book describing mankind's encounters with his Creator. The stories and people who made it into the Bible are not necessarily the who's-who of the human race. They are simply the ones God knew we would need to hear about and refer back to over and over in the ages to come, in order to help us

Whose story of waiting inspires you, and whose do you relate to the most?

better encounter Him in a personal way. They model hope, eternal strategies, and victorious lifestyles for us, and show us how long-suffering (patience on steroids) gets us ready for long-awaited, incredible blessings.

Why do you think the story of Daniel waiting and fasting to gain understanding of a vision was included?[17] The angel coming with the answer had been sent to Daniel the day Daniel (who was highly favored) had humbled himself and asked God for wisdom, but a demon prince delayed the angel 21 days. The story assures us that the devil can't stop

---

[17] See Daniel 10:2-12

an answer — only delay it. When God is about to release wisdom, blessings, or even a new assignment, most likely there will be opposition and delay. But be assured, nothing can keep God's Word from being ultimately accomplished. It never returns to Him empty, but always completes the purpose for which it was sent.[18] We may not have an awesome angelic being appear to us and explain the delay like the story of Daniel depicts for us, but his story gives us hope. Understanding that our prayers are heard the first moment our hearts whisper, "Father," means we can trust as we patiently wait that our answer may be delayed, but it's on the way!

Oh, wait a minute! I just thought of a fun kind of waiting: waiting with God. He just reminded me that by using the time to appreciate His company, we can enjoy the process no matter how long it takes. Reveling in the presence of your Heavenly Father, your Hero, your Inspiration, the One Who gave you your sense of humor and wired you to perceive what "fun" even means, is like turning the chore of waiting

---

[18] See Isaiah 55:11

into "a spoonful of sugar." Laugh with Him over silly things (like tapping your fingers impatiently waiting for the microwave) and see Him for Who He really is: our kind, joyful, patient, caring, empathetic Parent. Come to Him with your frustrations, impatience, and weaknesses, and discover His Potter's Hand that masterfully reshapes and smooths out any unwanted edges or unsealed cracks. Soak in His laughter and feel your strength rising, mountains crumbling, and impossibilities suddenly seeming possible.

Think about all the very best childhood moments you had with your favorite adults, then string them all together in your mind. Waiting with God is a billion times better. I know for some, thinking back can conjure up all kinds of sadness and regret, and I am so sorry. My guess would be that for you, enjoying God's company is something you've had to work really hard to do. But hard or easy, God wants us to delight in Him as much as He delights in us.

Before He created the world, He has loved and delighted in you even while you were just a twinkle in His Spirit, and your name was a favorite chapter title in His epic manuscript He was about to publish. God wanting you to glorify Him and enjoy Him is not for His sake;[19] it's for yours. Seeing Him with your childlike faith and playing together with Him in your imagination are some of the most wonderful "while you wait" experiences there are to have. When was the last time you laughed with God? You're probably due.

Okay, this may feel like a detour (and it actually is *about* a detour) but please go with me for a minute and I promise we'll end up back on track. I've always lived in New England. The Atlantic Ocean is a day trip for us. Every New England state is bordered by water. Even Vermont has the Connecticut River on the east side and Lake Champlain on the west. But as close as I live, I had not been to the ocean for over ten years. I wasn't really missing it. I'm more of a mountain person. I've always connected with the pine-scented forests and mountaintop vistas. But two autumns ago on our way to the mountains, we found ourselves just a few miles from the beach. It had been so long since we had seen the ocean, we decided to take a detour.

---

[19] See Malachi 1:6, Ephesians 1:3-14

5: From Waiting to Wanting

I didn't want to stop; it was too cold. Just a glance would be enough and we could be on our way.

As much as the ocean takes second place to the mountains for me, I felt strangely nostalgic as we turned down one of the many quaint and narrow beach roads lined with shuttered cottages and nautical décor. Then, something very unexpected happened as we pulled out onto the main road and the ocean sparkled its way into view — I cried. I asked my husband to roll down his driver side window closest to the ocean. The clapping waves, the salty air, and rhythmic surges, connected to my heart, and I cried. I didn't know how much I had missed the ocean until I saw its beauty and felt its music. The wait had been so long, I had shut that longing, that wanting, off. But the undetected desire hidden for years was still there. I wonder, how many other dreams and cries of our hearts have we silenced because the wait was too long?

Some of you who are reading this have been waiting for the answer to a certain need or a

How long is too long for you?

childhood dream for so long that you have given up. You've already beaten yourself up thinking you mustn't have had enough faith. You may have decided you weren't worthy to receive it from God anyway. Deep down, a part of you has declared that God doesn't understand how important it is for you to have this one thing or see it happen. Long-suffering may have proven good for Bible characters, but for you the suffering part has just proven *too* long. The conflict in your mind has forced you to shut off the "want."

Consider this God's gentle whisper of an invitation to your weary heart. It's time to delight yourself in His company. Come follow the narrow side road that leads to the beach. What you think is just a detour may actually be the Lord trying to reignite your "wanting" and restore your hope. He may even want to transform or redirect

Is there a special time or a place where you feel the closest to God?

your desire toward something that's even better for you than where your dreams were once headed.

When we long for His company most of all, everything else merely becomes stocking stuffers. As a middle-class American child on Christmas morning, after the one long-awaited big present finale had been unwrapped, and even though it was exactly what you had been hoping for, the opening-presents adrenaline was still pumping. It had to have been some brilliant parent who invented stocking stuffers to extend the gift-opening process, helping wean children off the excitement-frenzy, so they could actually eat Christmas breakfast without choking. There was something therapeutic about reaching into an oversized sock to pull out little surprises of inexpensive practical items like lip balm and travel-sized toothpaste, that somehow eased the dopamine withdrawal. The point I'm trying to make at the expense of embarrassing myself (admitting I can even relate to such over-indulgence) is that often what we think we just "hafta have" to be content, what we long for, beg for, and whine for the most, might possibly be caused by a chemical impulse.

What Now?

Whims are a fickle thing. They are the opposite of waiting. Impulse-buying can cause you to invest time or money into something that may cause an initial rush at the checkout, but any long-term payoff or promise of pleasure, falls flat and can lead to some major disappointments and financial struggles. In the heat of the moment though, shopping-adrenaline leaves no room for waiting because rationalization tells us: waiting will only increase the desire and I want this so badly I might just explode from anymore waiting-induced wanting. I better get it now.

Can we ever learn? For some it takes a significant loss. But we can start to curb our living at the mercy of whims just by being aware of them, their negative effects and "now or never" deception. You don't have to deny the purchase impulse altogether; you just need to learn to recognize it and work with it. One way to curb shopping urges is to put the "can't live without" item in your shopping cart for a while as you browse for real necessities (hopefully on your pre-made list). Then just before you go to the checkout, bring the gotta-have item back to its shelf or rack.

Pick it up and ask yourself if it still brings you joy, or is it meant to bring joy to someone else today? Put it on the shelf and if it hops back into your cart before you leave, take it home. If not, walk away knowing you just successfully took charge of that impulse. Congratulations!

Waiting can help determine if you really want it. Marketing strategists get it. They're human as well and understand our tendencies firsthand. That's why most impulse merchandise is placed at the checkout. It doesn't give you time to think, and imposes a sense of urgency. How many meltdowns have you seen at the checkout counter when candy or in demand items are being denied? The kicking, the tears, the desperate cries of "but I *neeeed* that!" and I'm not talking about toddlers here. Come on now, fess up. It's not just me. Your inner child pulls it on you too (does it not?). There's no waiting time to think it through or to weigh out pros and cons. It's an instant wide-eyed, mesmerizing (ooh pretty) fascination that makes all that is within you groan, "I ... must ... have ... that — *NOW!*" Who can resist a once in a lifetime offer like this for a limited time only, or so it feels? Tell me, who could possibly live without one of those cute little packs of pocket-sized tissues? It's a must have. Why, your nose practically starts running at the thought.

Not all impulses are bad. Most dreams and desires start as an impulse in the form of a want or a need. They are normal and natural and given to us so we can experience God's kindness, His character, and faithful provision. But just like curbing impulse buying by letting a gotta-have-it article ride around in our cart for a while, God will often make us wait for something we think we want, so that we can know for sure if we really *do* want it. Persevering through the lingering process of God's "Yes, but not yet," helps us be ready to receive it with a real appreciation and a clearer perspective of its proper place in our affections. Anything we want more than wanting God's best for us, has

Is there something you once thought you "had to have" but now you know differently?

90

the potential to pull us under. Every now and then, we have to stay in the store a very long time before we realize that what we thought we needed should actually get put back on the shelf for someone else to buy. More often than not, when we finally surrender it, God stuffs it in our stocking as a surprise. We thought we were waiting for God, but He was really waiting for us to "*seek Him first*" so we would be ready to have "*all these things added.*"[20]

Oh, by the way, the package did arrive today with the long-awaited birthday-money purchase. I knew you'd want to know that. It was glorious and cause for much celebratory skipping and jumping. I guess it's proof that...

Some things really can be worth the wait.

---

[20] See Matthew 6:33

Can you think of things that proved well worth your wait?

6:

From Closed to Closer

When the sign reads "Sorry, We're Closed," the doors are usually locked, and the lights are off inside. The customer may have all kinds of money to invest, but it's not going to happen until that sign gets turned around. It's hard to be open to dreaming again, to hear God's instructions, to let Him invest in you, when your heart is closed and the lights are turned off. The first sentence of Matthew 13:15 taps on our locked doors:

"For this people's heart has become calloused; they hardly hear with their ears and they have closed their eyes."

What Now?

Past disappointments, times of suffering, and being overwhelmed by darkness, can shut us down and lock us up. God wants to help us turn our "Open" signs back around again.

He loves to hide treasures for us to find. God knows we like games. We can't seek for treasure very well with our eyes (and hearts) shut. Making it a game helps coax them open. God often hides clues to follow in plain sight, so to speak, right under our noses, but camouflaged. You have to really focus to pick them out. It was God's idea to make it fun. Just look at Nature. Spots and stripes hide the hunter, as well as the hunted, though it was not God's intent for His Creation to have to hide from one another for fear of being eaten. Humankind closed down God's dream for us and quickly turned what was meant to be a relaxed, casual dining experience, into a serious life-or-death buffet. Up to the point of the Genesis flood, we were all vegetarians, including the animals.[21] It only makes sense to me that camouflage was originally

---

[21] Genesis 9:2-3

created just for the fun of it, and in God's Kingdom to come, harmony between all species will be restored, reinstating camouflage for hide and seek games, to be used solely for sport, not for survival. For now, hunting with a camera, tracking animals to capture a picture, following clues to get the best shot, is more my kind of game hunting fun. Does anyone else love following clues and searching for hidden treasure? I suppose one person's treasure could be another person's trash, but I'd like to think that discovering what you're looking for, in some way proves satisfying for just about everyone.

Growing up, I used to receive my monthly copy of a children's magazine, and for me the "hidden puzzle page" was the best of all the pages. It was the first page to which I'd turn. The artists who drew the puzzles were so clever. The lines of smaller drawn items were skillfully hidden within the bigger main picture by sharing some of the same drawn lines as that main picture. After finding all the items on the list, I'd look to my next favorite puzzle to find and circle all the subtle differences between two practically identical pictures. I've been known to give it a try even now, if the waiting room is empty and that still popular children's magazine is staring at me from amongst the others on the coffee table. There are some things you never outgrow.

There was another "best page," back in the day, when people's main source of daily news was printed on very large sheets of newspaper. Every day, morning and evening, news from around the nation and the world, and local news of sports, weather, movie times, human interest stories, obituaries, even wedding and birth announcements, were published for anyone with eyes to read. It was meant to be perused over with a morning cup of coffee or later with an evening dessert. But I'd always find myself furiously hunting through the folded sections of pages that had been delivered to my doorstep (or front hedges, or a nearby puddle) for that one significant page. I think you'll agree when I tell you which one. Amongst all the pages of words, teeming with their vast wealth of information, shone the brightest and most important page of all — The Comics! Am I right? It really was the only page that mattered. It even had word and number puzzles to solve. Some were tricky, but because the paper came every day you didn't have to wait too long for the answers. They were in the next day's edition, unless it was one of Saturdays' sadistically trickier puzzles that stumped you. They made them harder on purpose and then made you wait till Monday for the answers because Sundays' paper was a unique edition all to itself.

Unlike the rest of the weeks' measly two-sectioned newspaper, Sundays' edition had so many sections they needed to be lettered and put in a Table of Contents. This mega-version only came once a week, so mercifully the answers to Sundays' puzzles would be somewhere in that day's paper (because who could possibly wait seven whole days for that all important solution to the last, impossible to solve baffler?).

But the best thing of all about the Sunday newspaper was its entire section, not merely a page this time, a whole specially-folded insert devoted to "all that really mattered" to me. But wait, there's more. This all-important section was entirely in color! And they were not just like the ordinary weekday, meagerly 3-framed strip of black-and-white funnies. Oh no. On Sundays, they were practically graphic novels, each a half a page. It was its own section of large and in color comical hilarity. The editors were finally getting their priorities in line with mine.

Then in the 1990s, the color printing that made Sundays' edition of the comics so special, also made it possible to add to the back page of that section, a kind of "puzzle" that had to be in color to work. It was a computer-generated 3-D picture phenomenon visible

Have you ever noticed what you go to first, and wondered why that is?

only to those who knew the secret of relaxing their eyes to "out of focus" so that the hidden picture would "magically" come *into* focus. It was one of those things that had suddenly become quite popular. At first, I couldn't understand it at all; how staring at what appears to be blurry random dots and patterns on the page, could somehow cause a three-dimensional picture to emerge. If you didn't know how to do it, what the trick was, you could stare for hours and … nothing! As fascinating as the mystery was for most, it proved ridiculously frustrating for others, like me. Until one life-changing moment when someone suggested I cross my eyes as I looked at it. It was a way to relax my focus, and suddenly the eagle that was there all along, soared off the page at me. Once you learn the technique, you're always just seconds away from seeing a previously invisible world. It was eye opening.

God has amazing techniques to open us up to seeing the secrets of His invisible Kingdom. Stories told in precisely the right way can lead the listener into a whole different sphere. Jesus tells us quite a few stories and parables about treasures, seeking, and the Kingdom of God. *"So was fulfilled what was spoken through the prophet: 'I will open my mouth in parables, I will utter things hidden since the creation of the world.'"*[22] The phrase Jesus commonly used after hiding a golden nugget or two in His

---

[22] Matthew 13:35

teaching was, "He who has ears to hear, let him hear." In other words: For those who are really interested enough to understand this treasure hunt of a story, you can start looking now. It's like a "hidden picture puzzle" of finding the real story within the main storyline and then applying the truth by looking for all the subtle differences between the picture Jesus just painted and your own life, and circling what needs changing. When you trust in the mystery of Scripture being the Living Word of God and relax your focus, the truth of what you read there can soar off the page and bring you to that sudden "Aha!" moment of seeing a whole new realm.

We know that Jesus was often misunderstood, misquoted, and falsely accused, and yet it didn't stop Him from speaking figuratively or purposely in riddles. Jesus was God in the flesh, and God *invented* communication. He knew exactly what to do and say for His listeners to perfectly understand the intended meaning of His stories and statements. Why would He hide it from some, and make it so that only those "with ears to hear" could understand? Could it be, that like waiting for something reveals its importance to us, searching for the hidden meaning and then discovering it for ourselves actually increases its impact, becoming more memorable and meaningful to us?

Those with "ears to hear" may also indicate those who are "ready and willing" to follow through and obey Jesus' teaching. If He taught it  plainly (with no parables or hidden meanings), any people listening who were just curious and only looking to be entertained would be held accountable if they understood, and yet chose to ignore it. Hunger is a driving force designed to motivate us to action. Jesus knows only those hungry enough to seek out the meaning are ready and willing enough to apply His teaching to their lives. Out of kindness, He hides the meaning from the half-hearted listeners. When we seek with hopeful expectancy, hungry, ready and willing, we can be sure He will guide us to what was intentionally hidden for us to discover.

There was another kind of hide and seek game we used to play called "Hot or Cold." One person hides an object and then lets the seeker know if the direction they are heading in is closer to, or farther away from, the hidden object by saying: cold, colder, freezing (as the seeker progressively moves away from it), or warm, warmer, hotter, boiling hot (as they get closer and closer to the hidden object). The hint-giver has poetic license to invent creative terms as long as they indicate a drop or rise in temperature: polar bears, icebergs, lava hot, solar flares, etc. Maybe we were just easily amused. It was good for at least a half hour of entertainment on a rainy afternoon.

> *If we were playing "Hot or Cold" right now, how would you describe your "closeness" to God?*
>
> _____
>
> _____

Being able to hear the Holy Spirit's hints and indications that we are on the right path and heading in the right direction is a big part of moving from "Closed" to "Closer." Listening to Scripture and spending one-on-One time with the God who wants to reveal where our dreams have been

102

hiding, is a foundational practice for recognizing His voice and following His prompts. I sense we're getting warmer to seeing our dreams happen again. We've got our hands on that "Closed" sign, and we are that much closer to turning it around. He's always giving us hints. Keep listening. I think I may have just heard Someone say, "Melting popsicles."

Most people will admit that even as a grown-up there's something enjoyable about following clues and finding objects (except missing keys or wallets that you just had in your hand a minute ago and somehow ended up in the refrigerator or washing machine). Sure, hiding can be fun; even hiding things like Easter eggs or treasure hunt clues for others to find can be great. But even greater for me, is the "seeking and discovering" part. It's more gratifying. To resolve or uncover what was once concealed evokes a sense of victory.

There's nothing like a classic game of hide and seek. It's a good thing I have grandchildren. Can you imagine inviting my senior adult friends over to play?

What Now?

The challenge of it these days is finding a place that this older, larger adult body of mine can fit into, and even more importantly, get out of. Maybe that's why I'd rather seek. I must admit, pretending not to see those little 4-year-old feet sticking out in full view, "Where could he be?" accompanied by his hee-hee and a muffled whisper, "I'm over here," is not because I'm a nice grandmother; it's that it extends my time as the seeker, and postpones me having to squeeze into potentially imprisoning spaces.

The 6-year-old hider is still small enough to fit into all kinds of places, yet old enough to be very quiet, with no giggling or giving away her spot. I'm grateful for: "Alle, alle auch sind frei!" (or as we used to say it, "Olly-Olly-oxen-free!"). Roughly translated from its original German it means: "Everyone, everyone is free!" It's what a seeker yells when they give up, or someone makes it back to home base and that round is over. It signals to the rest of the hiders: You're free to come out from hiding now, and you won't be tagged or penalized. I have to tell you, it's a good fallback to have when your grandchild has vanished into thin air.

6: From Closed to Closer

But when it *is* my turn to hide (mostly behind floor length curtains or half open doors), as a grandparent, I'm sensitive to any younger seeker's attention span. If it's the 4-year-old seeking as opposed to the 13-year-old, I'm going to leave larger than life clues for him to find me. It's uncanny, but I always seem to "have to" clear my throat or cough, for some unknown reason, when the little one is looking. Strangely enough, it doesn't happen to me when the older ones are.

Would you rather hide or seek? Why is that?

God knows what our attention spans are better than we do. He understands a young, seeking heart can tire quickly. At times our loving Heavenly Father will clear His throat or cough a little to give away the hiding spot, so we don't give up looking altogether. As our faith matures, He'll increase the challenge for us to find what He's hidden. If He makes it too easy, it won't serve its purpose. I think I might have heard God's "Ahem" a minute ago when I was writing about Jesus speaking in parables. There may be some hints in His stories that could guide us to a better understanding of dreaming without dread. If we can really hear what God is saying to us, it might just lead us to some healing of past disappointments as well as the deferred hope that can creep in over time.

The parables in the 13th chapter of Matthew, compare the Kingdom of Heaven to being like a pearl of great price and like a treasure in a field. The discoverers of these incredible finds, sell everything they own, all that they have, to buy them. Their sacrificial purchases are often interpreted as our response to discovering God's Kingdom for ourselves. However, since it was Jesus Who sacrificially purchased *us*, wouldn't it be more likely that these stories should be understood from His perspective? Finding *you*, His treasure in a field and His pearl of great price, caused Him to give up all He had in Heaven, even His very life, to redeem you so He could call you His own.

Time and again, we miss the clues left for us in some of the very parables meant to reveal how precious we are to the God who made us. Jesus is like the shepherd in the 15th chapter of Luke, who left the whole herd in the pen to find the one who wandered away; and just like the woman who lost a valuable coin searched high and low, night and day, until she found it, He will pursue you. When each found what was lost, they called all their neighbors to rejoice with them and celebrate. Just like when one of us who has wandered away and fallen into doubt or unbelief has a change of heart, all of heaven rejoices. Can you see that you are that one? You have great value!

God wants you to know that *you* are His treasure. He is a Mighty King who lovingly pretends not to see us, but instead waits for us to surrender when we feel safe enough to come out from our hiding place. We hear Jesus calling, "Alle! Alle auch sind frei! Everyone! Everyone is free!" That round is over. It's safe now to come out from hiding. No one will be penalized. We want to believe it, it's just that we've been hiding in a cramped spot for so long it's hard to move and we can't seem to pry ourselves out of it. Looks like we could use a little help this time. Talking to a trusted counselor or wise friend is always a good place to start (I hope mine has a crowbar). Remember we are promised that with God nothing is impossible.

His love, poured into our souls by His Holy Spirit, assures us that it's okay to come out of hiding and to bring our dreams with us. We may want to bring our dreams along, but a stepped-on dream can be buried so deeply in a heart, and covered up with so much

Why do people bury treasure? Do you think it might be the same reason they bury their dreams?

disappointment and doubt, that digging it up feels impossible. It will take an expert Excavator to unearth it. Jesus doesn't care if it was *you* who buried the dream and threw away the map.

He wants you to know: *I hear your heart's cry and I know the suffering you've endured. I experienced it with you. My Spirit comforted you through it, remember? Here, take a sip of water and a deep breath. Feel My peace come over you.*

6: From Closed to Closer

The water is My Word, replenishing you,
and washing away any dirt thrown on you.
The breath you breathe in is Mine,
filling your spirit and reviving your hope.

My promises are like an oil of gladness;
a balm soothing the wounded warrior in you.
But also a refurbishing oil to restore you, polish you,
and make you shine like the Son again.

My Spirit has sealed you to My heart.
No amount of hiding or dirt thrown will ever change that.
The closer you come to Me, the more you will discover
My glory within you and see what a pearl of great price,
what a treasure you truly are to Me.

Open your eyes.
They were closed before from the pain,
but now open them to see the glorious treasure
that drawing near to Me has revealed.
It was hidden in you all along.

What Now?

Our Father's heart wants to pump life back into us and into our desire to dream with Him again. Jesus never leaves nor forsakes us;[23] even if we pull the shades, turn off the lights, and pretend we're not there, He understands why. And of course He knows just where we are. In fact, He's standing right there in the dark next to us whispering, "I'll wait right here with you until you're ready." So, what do you think? Are we ready?

His love has turned the lights back on allowing us to see that our dreams are still here. As our eyes adjust to the light of His love, and our focus relaxes knowing we're safe, we will see our dreams start to emerge off the page. They may have been camouflaged, but they were there all along. All we have to do now is turn the sign around to say...

"Yes, we're OPEN!"

---

[23] See Hebrews 13:5

7:

From Lost Glory to Last Glory

Dreaming and building with God is what we were created to do. We are actually here to fulfill *His* dream. We're His fearfully and wonderfully made creative building project. Still, we need the glory that was lost in the Garden of Eden to be personally restored to our individual lives before we can truly manifest God's vision. That glory, lost by Adam and Eve, was the radiant glory that had once clothed humanity from the inside out — the very power and visible presence of God. Surrendering their robes of righteousness to the serpent by doubting God's Character and intentions, they ignorantly surrendered all of our robes as well.

We all fall short of the glory God originally designed us to carry.[24] The Lord Jesus Christ was the only One who could reclaim our relinquished spiritual robes. The good news is: He did! He demonstrated God's love and real intentions — in that while we were still sinners, Christ died for us.[25]

Out of pure mercy, God graciously reinstates each who asks Him. As we trust in the sinless life-Blood Jesus shed in our behalf and believe that God raised Him from the dead, He brings us out of the kingdom of darkness and naked shame, and into His wonderful light.[26] Once again we are robed in spiritual glory and right standing with God; once more, able to dream with our Creator and fulfill *His* dream.

The dream He wants to birth through us will bring King Jesus so much glory, that for our entire lives the devil has been throwing all he can to deter it from coming true. Truth be told, the enemy can only delay God's dream. *We* are the only ones who can stop it

---

[24] See Romans 3:23
[25] See Romans 5:8
[26] See 1 Peter 2:9

from happening, by giving up or saying no. That's why it's so important not to lose hope. I know you are tired, but please don't give up. Be reinfused with the powerful Blood of Jesus and His holy, glorious, lifegiving Spirit. Experiencing His glory is why He made each of us as uniquely as He did. There are so many aspects of His glory to reflect, He needs all of us to absorb and reflect one sparkle of His brilliance at a time.

What would you say to someone who is about to give up on a dream?

"Glory" has almost become the buzz word these days among the modern prophets. Scripture tells us that Jesus gave apostles and prophets to His people so we can be prepared and united.[27] They are hearing from God that the days just ahead are promised to be some of the most glory-filled ever experienced by humanity.

---

[27] See Ephesians 4:11-13

What Now?

After recent events, it's hard to envision it, and I must confess it almost feels to me like wishful thinking.

I recently came across this journal entry of a conversation I had with God that made no sense to me at the time, but reading it now, I see this common thread God had woven into it for me to find and share with you. I don't consider myself a prophet, but I can see now how the Holy Spirit was clueing me in, back in October 2017, as to His apparent plans for us today:

Never have I been so perplexed by feelings of uncertainty. God, I know You told me that the heavens are open to me, and yet I stand here speechless, motionless, and uncertain of the space-time continuum. I can hardly spell it, never mind know what it means. What does it really mean?

God responded and I wrote it down:

Your mind is skipping rope double Dutch, getting all tangled, and giving up. Don't lose hope. Just dream and create. Close your eyes expecting a sunrise of colors, not a sunset. Beyond the ideas of yesterday. I'm taking you, and yours, beyond them — filled with My glory. They will be called "the Glory Days," filled with great exploits and adventures.

7: From Lost Glory to Last Glory

Joy and satisfaction will begin and end each day. No dread. No anguish. Only sweet expectation and supernatural strength. This is your time to keep your eyes to the path, enjoying the stillness, the fragrances, the significance of this catch-your-breath moment ... Another day you'll understand. It's only going to get bigger and better! Great exploits have begun, proportionately: Grace, Fun, Challenges, Miracles.

Four years later, I realize I still don't know what the space-time continuum really means. I remember decades ago, when trying to grasp the concept, that it felt like a mathematical word problem to me. I'm a word girl, not a math whiz. I talk my way out of math problems by finding a practical solution like, "Don't go by train then, just fly." I imagine that's why I shut down even trying to remember what this "spacey time-consuming" theory was. Today, after reading through many different sources, I am more confused than when I started. No wonder I never retained its definition. My research confirms that the space-time continuum is indeed mathematical. I knew it! What consoled me though was the last article I read. It assured me if I still didn't understand, not to feel too badly. There are scientists who don't fully comprehend the theory either. What did end up making sense to me, was that God had led my pen to write it down years ago because I was going to need to read it again now. It was His way of assuring me:

See, I told you way ahead of time so you'd know it was from Me, and that the glory to see miracles, signs and wonders is not just the prophets' wishful thinking. It really is coming. Keep dreaming and keep creating. I hold your future and I hold you. You don't have to fully understand how time and space are related — My heavenly realm is outside of them anyway — you only have to rest in My presence here and now.

God was already present "here and now" when He gave me that word way back "there and then." My numerically-challenged fallback has always been: I don't have to be gifted at math as long as I know someone who is. What He's saying to us is we don't need to know the "how to" and "whys" of our hopeful dreams, we just have to know the One who does.

We know that the once lost glory of Eden will be completely restored when King Jesus returns to Earth to reign, and our mortal bodies will be glorified to live forever just like His. But this "last glory" the prophets are talking about, is a supernatural manifestation of God's power displaying His character and love through miracles, signs and wonders. As it spreads globally, it will produce a unity of love between all Christ-followers that will catch the attention of unbelievers. Witnessing the "last glory" will draw so many people back to the Father through Jesus, that we will all be dancing in the streets positively giddy. We'll be ministering 24/7 purely strengthened by His joy. If it's anything like the prophet Haggai describes, the latter glory will be even greater than the former. Just listen to what the Lord promised His people in Haggai 2:3-9 regarding rebuilding the temple:

"Who of you is left who saw this house in its former glory? How does it look to you now? Does it not seem to you like nothing? ... Be strong, all you people of the land," declares the Lord, "and work. For I am with you ... My Spirit remains among you. Do not fear ... In a little while I will once more shake the heavens and the earth, the sea and the dry land. I will shake all nations, and the desired of all

*nations will come, and I will fill this house with glory ...
The silver is mine and the gold is mine ... The glory of this
present house will be greater than the glory of the former house
... And in this place, I will grant peace," declares the
Lord Almighty.*

Was the temple being described here in Haggai,
a foreshadow of God's dream for us? Are we the
"present house" of which the Lord Almighty was really
speaking? Hebrews 3:6 tells us that *"we are His house,
if we hold on to our courage and the hope of which we boast."*
Though presently scattered in earthen vessels all over
this planet, we are being prepared by the Father
through a mighty global shaking in order to hold the
latter glory like no man-built temple ever could.

A passage of Scripture stood out to me today as I was
spending time with God and reading through the book
of Romans. Two specific phrases were highlighted to
me, and I thought to myself He must purposely have
me reading the book of Romans in order to help me
fill the *space* of these very pages at this exact *time*, as
a *continuum* between lost glory and last glory:

Therefore, since we have been justified through faith, we have peace with God through our Lord Jesus Christ, through whom we have gained access by faith into this grace in which we now stand. **And we rejoice in the hope of the glory of God.** *Not only so, but we also rejoice in our sufferings, because we know that suffering produces perseverance; perseverance, character; and character, hope.* **And hope does not disappoint us,** *because God has poured out his love into our hearts by the Holy Spirit, whom he has given us.*[28]

Is God highlighting anything else to you?

There's something in this passage He wants us to unfold like a freshly cutout paper snowflake. The glory that is delicately folded up inside our hopeful dreams needs to be revealed. When we help fulfill God's dream for us, it brings Him glory and joy as well.

---

[28] Romans 5:1-5

What Now?

Getting a glimpse of that can encourage us to persevere and hang on to our hope. But first comes the cutting part. Got your scissors?

I know there are longer words to write (like "disappointment"), but writing out the 12 letters of "perseverance" actually makes me tired, and now I know why. Because according to this passage in Romans, perseverance is connected to suffering. Most people don't persevere through eating a delicious dessert, watching their favorite show, or taking a lazy summer afternoon nap in a hammock. Those only bring refreshment. Perseverance is supposed to bring us character. Can anybody tell me what "character" even is? And do we really need more of it? Whatever it is, how in the world does it produce hope? Please bear with me if the answers are glaringly obvious to you, but apparently, I'm being blinded by their glare at the moment.

First, let's snip away at the word "character." It usually refers to a person's disposition or quality. Someone "with character" could be described as even-tempered, genuine, and noble, displaying integrity and moral fiber, having strength and endurance. Endurance? That's pretty much interchangeable with perseverance, isn't it? Hmmm…

As I was pondering, my grandson walked into the room. So I asked 13-year-old Eli his thoughts on this whole concept of suffering, to perseverance, to character, to hope, and how he thinks it works. He insightfully replied, "Suffering that you have to persevere through, would lead to character and hope, because it makes you confident that you can fully trust Jesus' love, because of what He just got you through." I loved that. Fully trusting in Jesus' love because He walked with you and sustained you through the suffering, creates a hopeful confidence.

God gives us His Holy Spirit to live inside us so we can be confident of our adoption into His family, and that's glorious enough! But beyond that, Jesus in you (the hope of glory)[29] assures us of the promised outward glory we will one day carry — the visible power of God's manifest presence. That kind of glory

---

[29] See Colossians 1:27

only comes on us a little at a time, and it sounds like suffering with Jesus yet trusting in His love, is foundational to being able to hold it up securely.

Why not pour His glory on us all at once, free and easy, so we'd be good to go? We've all witnessed what happens to people that suddenly inherit great wealth or overnight popularity. They can end up so unraveled and confused. They don't know who their real friends are anymore, and can completely lose their own sense of value or importance. When the fame fades or the wealth quickly slips away, it's devastating. God's power displayed in us is meant to bring all credit and honor back to God. If too much of that power is bestowed on us before we're ready, we won't be able to carry it because we haven't developed the spiritual or emotional muscles to stand under its weight; the weight of possible fame, responsibility, our egos, or other people's jealous criticism, could prove overwhelming. If we were to experience glory all at once, we may even be tempted to take all the credit. We wouldn't have the humility and "God-confidence" gained by undergoing life's testing and trials.

7: From Lost Glory to Last Glory

How can we ready ourselves for this promised glory? We can't. Guess what it takes. Yup, that 12-letter word again. I wish it were easier, but our character can only be refined and strengthened the same way gold and precious metals are — in the fire. And we have to stay long enough in the fire of suffering to let it burn off impurities that would weaken us otherwise. When it's done its work, our character will be solidified with a stronger integrity than ever before, able to carry the intended glory God wants to fully restore to each of His devoted children.

Knowing what you know now, what would you tell your younger self?

It truly is in great love and care that the Holy Spirit walks us through the process, yet how hard it is for some of us to believe how loved we really are when we're in the middle of painful afflictions. Character-building can certainly feel like punishment in the moment. As much as there are times that we *do* suffer the consequences of our mistakes or wrong actions, and our character is built through the lesson learned, I think this verse is referring to a higher, more noble kind of suffering.

When we ache with the heart of Jesus for those around us, or feel the unfairness of others being mistreated, when our bodies suffer withstanding temptation, that's a more noble kind of suffering. A higher form of character comes when we suffer for doing what's right, for standing up for unpopular truth, and walking in paths of righteousness for His Name's sake. But Jesus promises us in Matthew 5:11-12:

Blessed are you when people insult you, persecute you and falsely say all kinds of evil against you because of me. Rejoice and be glad, because great is your reward in heaven…

Blessed is another way of saying "deeply happy." The last time you were left out or falsely gossiped about for being preachy or holier than thou, did it make you happy? Matthew 5:12 continues: "*Rejoice and be glad …*

for in the same way, they persecuted the prophets who were before you." The persecuted prophets were those who spoke the Words of God to the people. Is that why you find yourself suffering? Rejoice and be glad. How do we do that when our world is being shaken and our dreams are being dismantled by criticism? For the joy set before Him Jesus endured the Cross, scorning its shame.[30] Talk about someone's world being shaken while dreams crumble around them. He did that for us! We were part of the "joy set before Him." Knowing that the suffering ahead of Him would enable us to experience His Father's love and His intended glory for us, Jesus persevered.

Justified freely by God's grace through the redemption that came by Christ Jesus,[31] we can now confidently hope to have the complete glory God intended us to have before it was lost. Beyond our Blood-bought robes of righteousness that cover our shame, the Father's Holy Spirit is clothing us with

---

[30] See Hebrew 12:2
[31] See Romans 3:24

radiant ever-increasing glory from the inside out, piece by piece — from glory to glory.

Aha, so *that's* why we can rejoice in suffering. It's for glory's sake. I think I finally got it. If we know that our character is being strengthened by suffering in order to carry the glory God promised, we get more hopeful, knowing each day we endure makes us more ready for the "last glory!" Character produced through suffering really *can* produce hope. Who would have thought? I know it took me long enough, but thanks for persevering with me.

I'm being awed by the kindness of God and the impossible intricacies of His Creation every day. I just can't fathom that there could be more glory to come to this earth. I was recently looking at some roses that I had received as a gift. I had just finished reading the parable in Mark 4:26-29 about the Kingdom of God being like when a man scatters seed on the ground and whether he sleeps or gets up, night and day the seed sprouts and grows even though the man has no idea how. *"All by itself the soil produces grain — first the stock, then the head, then the full kernel in the head."*

If that isn't displaying the glory of God, I don't know what is. I glanced at my roses and thought about how each stem produced the leaves and then got bigger until somehow, the cells reproducing and growing, having the specific design of this particular yellow and pink rose encoded in each, produced just the right sequence to form buds that knew how to blossom, each one designed just a little differently. One single rose in itself is incredible, but as a bouquet they fill the room with their presence — a heavenly fragrance.

I've already experienced the weightiness of God's presence and felt humbled and unable to get off the floor. I've sensed His comfort and tangible arms of love wrapped around me. I have seen miracles of physical healing happen in front of me that reveal the Character of God — His healing love. I've witnessed people entrapped by fear and demonic oppression delivered and made whole by the authority Jesus has given us. His Name is glorified because God's Almighty power flows through that Name. The earth is already filled with so much of God's glory. We're hosting the Holy Spirit within us. What could be greater than this taste of heavenly power and divine understanding of the Father's ineffable love?

What kind of glory could possibly outshine that? Maybe one where all the sparkles of His glory are reflected back to Him all at once through us, together. We can't stare at the sun, but we can be mesmerized by the beauty of a sparkling lake. People walking in darkness can't bear to look at God's glory directly, but maybe we can be the ones to sparkle all together and reflect His beauty for them.

Much of what we've been experiencing lately has been God's covert operation of shaking us into position to better fit with a God appointed team of dream-buddies — our very own sparkling dream team. Those crumpled up hopes and ideas can be better reformed and revived with the shining support of fellow visionaries. The way God choreographs things, it would not surprise me if your dream and mine, both turn out to miraculously fit together somehow in a supernatural way. My prayer for us reflects one of Paul's blessings:

7: From Lost Glory to Last Glory

May the God who gives endurance and encouragement give us a spirit of unity among ourselves as we follow Christ Jesus, so that with one heart and mouth we may glorify the God and Father of our Lord Jesus Christ.[32]

Does God really have to shake us like this though? If you want to make space for more cookies to fit into a container, what do you do? You shake it down, right? [Okay, maybe you just eat a few, but that doesn't help me make my point.] Individually, He's been increasing our capacity to hold more of His glory, more of His power, so that as a company of glory carriers all fitting together, we can shine beyond the sun and see dreams happen, united for *His* glory, not ours. By dreaming with Him as a team, we are helping complete His dream even more. When each part of what the prophets are seeing comes together in completeness, the empowerment of God's Spirit, and His glory that we will be carrying, will melt away all memories of any suffering past or present. Only the character it produced and the glory of a hope fulfilled will remain.

---

[32] See Romans 15:5-6

What Now?

It's all so beyond me. And that's okay. I don't have to fully understand it all, because I know Someone Who does.

Oh, the depth of the riches of the wisdom and the knowledge of God! How unsearchable his judgment, and his paths beyond tracing out! Who has known the mind of the Lord? Or who has been his counselor? Who has ever given to God, that God should repay him? For from him and through him and to him are all things…

To Him be the glory forever! Amen.[33]

CONCLUSION:
From There to Here

The resistance training, and lessons of listening continued as I sat there taking dictation, waiting for a whole book to unfold in front of me; dreaming if I obediently kept scribbling words page by page, clear instructions and profound truths would suddenly appear. There have been times that the pieces of paragraphs scattered throughout a notebook full of frenzied writing have looked to me like they were all from different jigsaw puzzles sinisterly mixed together in one box. I wanted to throw them all out the window (along with the butterflies of inspiration) quite a few times. But this one thought pulled be back each time:

What Now?

I didn't ask to write this book. I heard God give me the title. He chose me to write this book; a book about dreaming again with Him, of all things! If He planted this dream in me, He will make it happen. My job is to simply keep writing. He'll tell me when it's done.

And here we are. I think He just gave me the signal. He pointed out to me that the last few paragraphs of Chapter 7, were filled with metaphors of "Sunshine and Roses." In case you skip over book introductions (like me), that's right where we began. I have about a chapter's worth of extra puzzle pieces all typed in to this laptop, but it sounds like those pages will be part of the next writing venture. Twice before, as I've come to the conclusion of writing a book, God has given me my next assignment by planting a title in my head. It's like telling a woman in the final stages of labor you have to do this all over again as soon as you finish. This time though, I have a prewritten chapter as well as the book's working title: *Dreaming with God.*

The fight to maintain a positive outlook is daily. As long as there are negative voices, ideas, and circumstances, there will be the need for fighting back with optimistic counterattacks. It may feel like war, but we can take the warship, turn it into worship, and discover that praising God, being thankful, and talking with others about God (about His goodness, beauty, provision, faithfulness, grace and mercy), not only helps cancel out the negativity and launched missiles, but it boomerangs them back from whence they came. I believe sharing in this process together, is God giving us a glimpse of *His* sweet dream for all of us.

Like so many times before, as I have released these words onto the pages (butterflies into the atmosphere) something within me has changed. I'm praying that as you've read and asked, *What Now?* you too, are inspired to try again, to hope again, and to dare enough to let yourself dream again.

It was years ago He told me He was taking us beyond the ideas of yesterday into "the Glory Days," filled with great exploits and adventures. That sounds like something God would dream up for us, doesn't it? Are you ready to give it another try? No more dreading. From here on, only glorious dreaming with the Giver of dreams, who is tenderly saying to each of us:

What Now?

I've loved you with an everlasting Father's love. Long before you were created, I knew you would need proof of that. Your spirit is too wobbly and woozy to stand up and grab it on your own. You needed some lifeblood to strengthen your ability to understand and take it for yourself. I breathed life into your lungs. And I'm breathing life into your spirit even as you read this. Receive My unconditional love and hugs and kisses of approval — A Father's love like no other.

Your future is resting with Me until you're ready to say "yes" again. Rededicate your life to My plan for you. You think you heard me tell you once how to solve "your need to know." I did. It was Me. But here we are again. You've forgotten how. It's knowing that I'm here with you, remember? From the inside out, I'm wholeheartedly supporting you in this next endeavor. And I AM with you. That's all "you need to know."

I gave you that idea, that dream. Don't tuck it away. Don't explain it away or disregard it altogether because of fear and the impossible length of rope binding up your adventurous spirit. Your time to dance, free and uninhibited, is here. I'm burning the ropes off of you with My fire of seeming affliction. I'm in the furnace with you. You will not be burned or consumed. Only the demons that have been holding you back will be incinerated.

CONCLUSION: From There to Here

Take a deep breath now. Not even the smell of smoke is on you. My love is filling up all the spots affected by the trials of refinement. Rejoice! The suffering led you to a perseverance that has produced character and integrity; the kind that will carry My glory to the nations. Get ready to receive My love and be emboldened to love others. I will give you the eyes to see who is next. Simply keep asking Me...

"Okay, God, what now?"

About the Author

For the past 30 years, Sue and her husband, Steve, have served in church leadership and ministry. She is a mother of two and a grandmother of five. She and Steve lived in central Massachusetts until 2014 when they moved to be near family in Connecticut. As lifelong New Englanders, their passion has always been to see God's Kingdom break ground in the very unique and often hardened soil of New England.

Sue has been creatively writing her whole life. Her ability was recognized early on by her teachers who unexpectedly presented her with a creative writing award at graduation. And though she did not pursue writing as a career, she did not let her gift go to waste. Over the years, she has been encouraged by many to publish her works of stage productions, children's church-curriculum, and live sermon illustrations (dramatic and comedic sketches), but the timing just didn't seem right to her — until recently.

God directed her to publish her first book (*Get Back on the Horse? GOD, You Can't Be Serious!*) in October 2019. After miraculously surviving childhood cancer, marrying her high school sweetheart, raising a daughter and son, ministering 25 years in different capacities at a local church, enduring seven years of care-giving for her parents (her mom having Alzheimer's); after being molded by some very traumatic life events, and then living through the pain of being pulled out of a very close-knit, conservative church family to pursue the supernatural gifts and calling of the Holy Spirit; after all of that, Sue was finally ready to publish her work. *Get Back on the Horse?* included many of her previous works, but turned out to be a culmination of the healing and recovery process God had laid out for her to walk through one page at a time.

Then just before publishing it, she woke up one morning to a dream-like vision of a church building rolling by on wagon wheels and hearing only the title, *Be on Your Way,* she knew she needed to begin writing her second book. With no idea where the book (or God) was taking her, she listened chapter by chapter for God's dictation, and wrote down what she thought she heard; nine months of writing later, it was complete (June 2020). Just days after publishing it, she heard the title of her next book: *What Now? From Dreading to Dreaming.* And so she continued to write on, in obedience to Inspiration.

Available at Amazon.com

Get Back
on the Horse?

GOD, You Can't be Serious!

Life is hard. So is the ground. One minute you're whistling along and then, BAM! As if time skipped a beat without telling you, you're lying there in disbelief, praying if you don't try to get up maybe nothing will hurt. But the ground feels so much harder than it used to, and it looks like your boot straps are all but worn out. We all can use a hand up once in a while.

This collection of encouraging stories, scripts, poems, and prayers is meant to breathe life into weary travelers and give a leg up to those who know it's time to get back on the horse (even though the saddle seems too high off the ground).

If you think for now, you'd just rather walk, be assured you're not alone. And with each step taken and each page turned, you're that much closer to being ready to mount up again…

but this time with wings as eagles.

Be on Your Way

Ready... Get set... Um... What comes next?

If you're a spiritually sensitive person you may have been feeling for a while now that something has shifted in the atmosphere, that something new and unprecedented is about to start, and you are not quite sure what your next step should be. *Be on Your Way* was written to assure you that you are not the only one wondering:

"On my way to where?"

There is a global move of God happening, and chapter by chapter this book suggests and unfolds ideas of where God may be headed and what we might need to pack or unload, hold onto or let go of, in order to freely move ahead unencumbered by past trips.

Be on Your Way takes you on the author's nine-month writing trek that prepared her (and possibly you as you read it) for the actual divine excursion ahead. It's a book to read while you're waiting patiently to board, not quite sure of your destination or your departure time, but knowing that you heard the call, too, and you want to be...

READY, and all SET... to GO!

141

Made in the USA
Middletown, DE
05 August 2021

45463453R00092